International Dimensions of

HUMAN RESOURCE MANAGEMENT

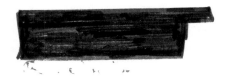

THE KENT INTERNATIONAL DIMENSIONS
OF BUSINESS SERIES

International Dimensions of
HUMAN RESOURCE MANAGEMENT

Peter J. Dowling
Monash University, Australia

Randall S. Schuler
New York University

THE KENT INTERNATIONAL DIMENSIONS OF BUSINESS SERIES
David A. Ricks
Series Consulting Editor

PWS-KENT Publishing Company
Boston, Massachusetts

This book is dedicated to all those who teach, practice, and support the understanding and advancement of international human resource management, particularly Leonard N. Stern, benefactor of the Stern School of Business, New York University.

Editor: Rolf Janke
Assistant Editor: Kathleen M. Tibbetts
Production Supervisor/Text Designer: Elise Kaiser
Cover Designer: Julie Gecha
Manufacturing Coordinator: Marcia A. Locke

PWS-KENT
Publishing Company

20 Park Plaza
Boston, Massachusetts 02116

PWS-KENT Publishing Company is a division of Wadsworth, Inc.

Printed in the United States of America.
  2   3   4   5   6   7   8   9 — 94   93   92   91   90

Library of Congress Cataloging-in-Publication Data

Dowling, Peter.
    International dimensions of human resource management / Peter J.
Dowling, Randall S. Schuler.
        p.   cm.—(The Kent international dimensions of business
series)
    Includes bibliographical references.
    ISBN 0–534–91946–4
    1. International business enterprises—Personnel management.
I. Schuler. Randall S.   II. Title.   III. Series.
HF5549.D627   1990   89–23100
658.3—dc20   CIP

Series Foreword

Prior to World War II, the number of firms involved in foreign direct investment was relatively small. Although several U.S. companies were obtaining raw materials from other countries, most firms were interested only in the U.S. market. This situation changed, however, during the 1950s—especially after the creation of the European Economic Community. Since that time, there has been a rapid expansion in international business activity.

The majority of the world's large corporations now perform an increasing proportion of their business activities outside their home countries. For many of these companies, international business returns over one-half of their profits, and it is becoming more and more common for a typical corporation to earn at least one-fourth of its profits through international business involvement. In fact, it is now rather rare for any large firm not to be a participant in the world of international business.

International business is of great importance in most countries, and that importance continues to grow. To meet the demand for increased knowledge in this area, business schools are attempting to add international dimensions to their curricula. Faculty members are becoming more interested in teaching a greater variety of international business courses and are striving to add international dimensions to other courses. Students, aware of the increasing probability that they will be employed by firms engaged in international business activities, are seeking knowledge of the problem-solving techniques unique to international business. As the American Assembly of Collegiate Schools of Business has observed, however, there is a shortage of available information. Most business textbooks do not adequately consider the international dimensions of business, and much of the supplemental material is disjointed, overly narrow, or otherwise inadequate in the classroom.

This series has been developed to overcome such problems. The books are written by some of the most respected authors in the various areas of international business. Each author is extremely well known in the Academy of International Business and in his or her other professional academies. They possess an outstanding knowledge of their own subject matter and a talent for explaining it.

These books, in which the authors have identified the most important international aspects of their fields, have been written in a format that facilitates their use as supplemental material in business school courses. For the most part, the material is presented by topic in approximately the same order and manner as it is covered in basic business textbooks. Therefore, as each topic is covered in the course, material is easily supplemented with the corresponding chapter in the series book.

The Kent International Dimensions of Business Series offers a unique and much needed opportunity to bring international dimensions of business into the classroom. The series has been developed by leaders in the field after years of discussion and careful consideration, and the timely encouragement and support provided by the PWS-KENT staff on this project. I am proud to be associated with this series and highly recommend it to you.

David A. Ricks

Consulting Editor to the
*   Kent International Dimensions of Business Series*
Professor of International Business,
*   University of South Carolina*

Preface

The globalization of business is having a significant impact upon human resource management. Europe 1992 is heightening this impact tremendously. It is more imperative than ever before for organizations to engage in human resource management on an international scale. Decisions have to be made concerning (1) the numbers and proportions of host-country nationals, third-country nationals, and expatriates in staffing plants and offices all over the world; (2) where and how to recruit these individuals and how to compensate them for their performance; and (3) whether personnel practices will be uniform across all locations or will be tailored to each location. While sometimes these decisions are partially answered by the strategy and structure decisions made by the organization, there still remains a great deal of latitude in the design of the final package of international human resource management practices.

International Dimensions of Human Resource Management touches upon human resource practices in many of the countries of the world. The primary focus of the book, however, is on the choices of international human resource management practices that confront multinational corporations and some factors to consider in making those choices.

The book is organized into eight chapters, one appendix, and a glossary. Chapter 1 begins with a description of international human resource management and what differentiates it from domestic human resource management. Chapter 2 examines the many aspects of international human resource planning, including the impact of the strategy and structure of multinational corporations (MNCs) on those aspects. Recruitment and selection of international employees are the focus of Chapter 3, with particular attention given to expatriates and the process of repatriation. Chapter 4 identifies the issues and choices in international performance appraisal and Chapter 5 discusses the dimensions of international training and development. Chapter 6 covers the many issues and dimensions of international compensation with numerous comparisons of pay practices across nations. Chapter 7 reveals the complexities and differences in labor relations when operating as an MNC. Chapter 8 is an epilogue describing the state of practice of international human resource management and an identification of the major associations dedicated to advancing the field. The appendix discusses the thorny and challenging research issues and dimensions of international human resource management. Finally, the extensive glossary presents and defines approximately 250 terms unique to this evolving field.

This book is written for the student of international human resource management and the practicing human resource manager who is involved in, or about to become involved in, international human resource management issues. As the world becomes more the global village, it is imperative for students and managers to familiarize themselves with the human resource practices in other countries. Additionally, as more U.S. based organizations become multinational, it is important to know the dimensions and choices associated with managing human resources in a multinational corporation.

Acknowledgments

Because out intent was to prepare a book that is useful for students and practitioners alike, we sought the input of both managers practicing international human resource management and academics teaching and researching international human resource management. We are grateful for the assistance of members of the International Chapter of the Society for Human Resource Management (formerly ASPA/I). Patrick Morgan, the 1989 President of the International Chapter of the Society for Human Resource Management, Dan Kendall of Rohm and Hass, and Marcus Moore of New York University were particularly helpful in the design of a survey questionnaire that we sent out to the ASPA/I membership. The responses to this questionnaire proved to be invaluable in offering insights into and providing examples of international human resource management choices and dimensions.

We were also aided from beginning to end by the fine review comments of several outstanding academics: Lee Dyer, Cornell University;

Mark A. Mendenhall, University of Tennessee, Chattanooga; Nancy K. Napier, Boise State University; Anne Tsui, University of California, Irvine.

Patrick Morgan provided many excellent review comments on the final draft of the manuscript. He also prepared the glossary that appears at the end of this book, which he developed in order to facilitate communication about the new and different ideas and concepts in international human resource management.

We also gratefully acknowledge the work of Helen De Cieri and Denice Welch of Monash University for their detailed critique of the final draft. The support and encouragement of Allan Fels, Director of the Graduate School of Management at Monash University; Richard West, Dean of the Stern School of Business at New York University; and Oscar Ornati, chair of the Management Area at New York University are greatly appreciated.

We also appreciate the capable secretarial assistance of Lillian Murphy at Monash University and Marci Winward at New York University.

We thank Rolf Janke and Kathleen Tibbetts at PWS-KENT Publishing Company for working with us and getting the book into its final form. They did a great job with the book, as they have with all the international books in this series edited by David Ricks. We also owe our thanks to David for letting us be a part of the fine series he has assembled with and for PWS-KENT.

Some of the preliminary research for this book was done while Peter Dowling was on sabbatical leave during 1985–85 at the New York State School of Industrial and Labor Relations at Cornell University. Our collaboration on this book began in late 1987 and continued with meetings on both sides of the Pacific during 1988 and 1989 and heavy use of the fax machine. The encouragement and assistance of Lee Dyer, George Milkovich, Barry Gerhart, John Boudreau, and Sara Rynes at Cornell University are much appreciated. We were also greatly aided by the wisdom and insights of Jean Benjamin Stora at HEC in France, Albert Stähli and Hans Zink at GSBA in Zürich, Shoji Matsumura at Sumitomo Bank in Tokyo, and Simcha Ronen at Tel Aviv University.

Finally, we wish to thank Fiona Dowling and Susan Jackson for their help and encouragement throughout this project.

Peter J. Dowling
Randall S. Schuler

About the Authors

PETER J. DOWLING (Ph.D., The Flinders University of South Australia) is Associate Director of the Graduate School of Management at Monash University, Melbourne, Australia. Previous teaching appointments include the California State University at Chico, the University of Melbourne, and Cornell University. He has also worked for Telecom Australia and the Royal Australian Air Force. His current research interests are concerned with the cross-national transferability of HRM practices and the HR implications of European integration in 1992. Professor Dowling has co-authored two books (*Personnel/Human Resource Management in Australia* with Randall Schuler and John Smart and *People in Organizations: An Introduction to Organizational Behavior in Australia* with Terence Mitchell, Boris Kabanoff, and James Larson). He has also written or co-authored over twenty journal articles and book chapters. He serves on the Editorial Board of *Human Resource Planning* and is the Editor of *Asia Pacific HRM*. He is National Junior Vice President of the Institute of Personnel Management Australia, and a member of the International Chapter of the Society for Human Resource Management, the Academy of Management, the Australian and New Zealand Association of Management Educators, the Academy of International Business, and the International Industrial Relations Association.

RANDALL S. SCHULER (Ph.D., Michigan State University) is Research Professor, Stern School of Business, New York University. His interests are international human resource management, organizational uncertainty, personnel and human resource management, entrepreneurship, and the interface of competitive strategy and human resource management. He has authored and edited twenty books, has contributed over twenty chapters to reading books, and has published over seventy articles in professional journals and academic proceedings. His current research interests are concerned with studying how companies align their human resource practices with strategy. Presently, he is on the Editorial Board of *Academy of Management Executive, Human Resource Management, Journal of Management,* and *Organization Science.* He is a Fellow of the American Psychological Association. Professor Schuler has been on the faculties of the University of Maryland, Ohio State University, Penn State University, and Cleveland State University. He also worked at the U.S. Office of Personnel Management in Washington, D.C. and has done extensive consulting and management development work in North America, Europe, and Australia.

Contents

CHAPTER 1

▼

Introduction and Overview

▲

Globalization is a dramatic new trend in international business. Many companies outside the United States have globalized their operations. For example, a recent listing by *Fortune* magazine showed that of the world's fifty largest industrial corporations, thirty-one have their headquarters outside the United States[1] (see Exhibit 1–1). A listing of the 100 biggest industrial corporations in the world shows that the United States dominates with 39, followed by Japan with 15 and West Germany with 12. In all, 15 countries are represented in the top 100. By contrast, of the fifty largest commercial banks in the world, Japan heads the list with twenty-three; the United States has just four (Citicorp, Chase Manhattan, J. P. Morgan, and Bank of America). Of the fifty, twenty are in Europe, twenty-five are in Asia, and four are in North America.

These data clearly show that the globalization of business has not been restricted to a handful of countries — it is an international trend. Companies that wish to compete successfully in world markets need to develop an international orientation. With respect to human resource management (HRM), Duerr[2] has noted:

> virtually any type of international problem, in the final analysis, is either created by people or must be solved by people. Hence, having

1

EXHIBIT 1–1 The Top 50 Industrial Corporations

1988 Rank	Company	Headquarters	Industry	Sales ($ Millions)	Profits ($ Millions)
1	General Motors	Detroit	Motor Vehicles	121,085.4	4,856.3
2	Ford Motor	Dearborn, Mich.	Motor Vehicles	92,445.6	5,300.2
3	Exxon	New York	Petroleum Refining	79,557.0	5,260.0
4	Royal Dutch/Shell Group	London/The Hague	Petroleum Refining	78,381.1	5,238.7
5	International Business Machines	Armonk, N.Y.	Computers	59,681.0	5,806.0
6	Toyota Motor	Toyota City (Japan)	Motor Vehicles	50,789.9	2,314.6
7	General Electric	Fairfield, Conn.	Electronics	49,414.0	3,386.0
8	Mobil	New York	Petroleum Refining	48,198.0	2,087.0
9	British Petroleum	London	Petroleum Refining	46,174.0	2,155.3
10	IRI	Rome	Metals	45,521.5	921.9
11	Daimler-Benz	Stuttgart	Motor Vehicles	41,817.9	953.1
12	Hitachi	Tokyo	Electronics	41,330.7	989.0
13	Chrysler	Highland Park, Mich.	Motor Vehicles	35,472.7	1,050.2
14	Siemens	Munich	Electronics	34,129.4	757.0
15	Fiat	Turin	Motor Vehicles	34,039.3	2,324.7
16	Matsushita Electric Industrial	Osaka	Electronics	33,922.5	1,177.2
17	Volkswagen	Wolfsburg (W. Ger.)	Motor Vehicles	33,696.2	420.1
18	Texaco	White Plains, N.Y.	Petroleum Refining	33,544.0	1,304.0
19	E.I. Du Pont de Nemours	Wilmington, Del.	Chemicals	32,514.0	2,190.0
20	Unilever	London/Rotterdam	Food	30,488.2	1,485.6
21	Nissan Motor	Tokyo	Motor Vehicles	29,097.1	463.0
22	Philips' Gloeilampenfabrieken	Eindhoven (Netherlands)	Electronics	28,370.5	477.1
23	Nestlé	Vevey (Switzerland)	Food	27,803.0	1,392.7
24	Samsung	Seoul	Electronics	27,386.1	464.3
25	Renault	Paris	Motor Vehicles	27,109.7	1,496.7
26	Philip Morris	New York	Tobacco	25,860.0	2,337.0

1988 Rank	Company	Headquarters	Industry	Sales ($ Millions)	Profits ($ Millions)
27	Toshiba	Tokyo	Electronics	25,440.8	438.9
28	ENI	Rome	Petroleum Refining	25,226.8	917.3
29	Chevron	San Francisco	Petroleum Refining	25,196.0	1,768.0
30	BASF	Ludwigshafen (W. Ger.)	Chemicals	24,960.5	802.2
31	Hoechst	Frankfurt	Chemicals	23,308.1	1,037.8
32	Peugeot	Paris	Motor Vehicles	23,249.7	1,485.8
33	Bayer	Leverkusen (W. Ger.)	Chemicals	23,025.9	1,055.5
34	Honda Motor	Tokyo	Motor Vehicles	22,236.5	819.5
35	CGE (Cie Générale d'Électricité)	Paris	Scien. & Photo. Equip.	21,487.5	362.4
36	Elf Aquitaine	Paris	Petroleum Refining	21,175.0	1,209.9
37	Amoco	Chicago	Petroleum Refining	21,150.0	2,063.0
38	Imperial Chemical Industries	London	Chemicals	20,839.0	1,490.9
39	NEC	Tokyo	Electronics	19,626.1	183.4
40	Occidental Petroleum	Los Angeles	Food	19,417.0	302.0
41	Procter & Gamble	Cincinnati	Soaps, Cosmetics	19,336.0	1,020.0
42	Ferruzzi Finanziaria	Ravenna	Chemicals	18,311.1	425.6
43	United Technologies	Hartford	Aerospace	18,087.8	659.1
44	Atlantic Richfield	Los Angeles	Petroleum Refining	17,626.0	1,583.0
45	Asea Brown Boveri	Zurich	Indus. and Farm Equip.	17,562.0	386.0
46	Daewoo	Seoul	Electronics	17,251.2	33.3
47	Nippon Steel	Tokyo	Metals	17,108.9	291.7
48	Eastman Kodak	Rochester, N.Y.	Scien. & Photo. Equip.	17,034.0	1,397.0
49	Boeing	Seattle	Aerospace	16,962.0	614.0
50	RJR Nabisco	Atlanta	Food	16,956.0	1,393.0

SOURCE: *Fortune* © 1989 The Time Inc. Magazine Company. July 31, 1989, p. 282.

3

the right people in the right place at the right time emerges as the key to a company's international growth. If we are successful in solving that problem, I am confident we can cope with all others.

The objective of this book is to analyze the process of internationalization by examining the international dimensions of HRM. In this first chapter, we shall define international HRM and examine the similarities and differences between domestic and international HRM.

DEFINING INTERNATIONAL HRM

Before we can offer a definition of international HRM, we should first define the general field of HRM. In general, HRM refers to those functions undertaken by an organization to effectively utilize its human resources. These functions would include at least the following:

▸ Human resource planning
▸ Staffing
▸ Performance evaluation
▸ Training and development
▸ Compensation
▸ Labor relations

We can now consider the question of which functions change when HRM goes international. A recent paper by Morgan[3] on the development of international HRM is helpful in considering this question. His paper presents a model of international HRM that is shown in Figure 1–1. His model consists of three dimensions:

1. The three broad human resource functions of procurement, allocation, and utilization.

2. The three national or country categories involved in international HRM activities: (1) the host country where a subsidiary may be located, (2) the home country where an international company is headquartered, and (3) "other" countries that may be the source of labor or finance.

3. The three types of employees of an international enterprise: (1) local/host-country nationals (HCNs); (2) expatriates/parent-country nationals (PCNs); and (3) third-country nationals (TCNs). Thus, for example, IBM employs Australian residents (HCNs) in its Australian operations, often sends U.S. employees (PCNs) to Australia on assignment, and may

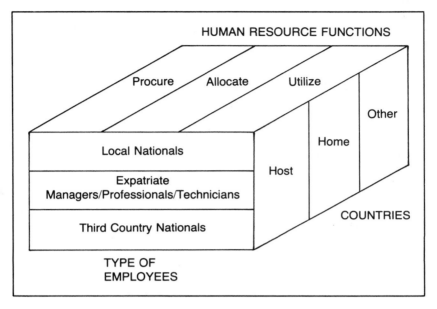

FIGURE 1-1 Model of International HRM

SOURCE: P. V. Morgan, "International Human Resource Management: Fact or Fiction," *Personnel Administrator*, Vol. 31, No. 9 (1986), p. 44. Reprinted from the Sept. 1986 issue of *Personnel Administrator* © 1986, The American Society for Personnel Administration, Alexandria, VA.

send some of its Australian employees on an assignment to its Japanese operations (as TCNs).

Morgan defines international HRM as the interplay among these three dimensions—human resource functions, types of employees, and countries of operation. We can see that in broad terms international HRM involves the same functions as domestic HRM (the three broad functions listed by Morgan can be easily expanded into the six HR functions listed above). The latter, however, is involved with employees within only one national boundary.

The complexities of operating in different countries and employing different national categories of workers are the main factors that differentiate domestic and international HRM, rather than any major differences between the HRM functions performed. Many companies underestimate the complexities involved in international operations, and there is some evidence to suggest that business failures in the international arena may often be linked to poor management of human resources. Desatnick and Bennett[4] conducted a detailed case study of a large U.S. multinational company and concluded:

> the primary causes of failure in multinational ventures stem from a lack of understanding of the essential differences in managing human resources, at all levels, in foreign environments. Certain management philosophies and techniques have proved successful in the domestic environment: their application in a foreign environment too often leads to frustration, failure and underachievement. These "human" considerations are as important as the financial and marketing criteria upon which so many decisions to undertake multinational ventures depend.

Increasingly, domestic HRM is taking on some of the flavor of international HRM as it deals more and more with a multicultural workforce. Thus, some of the current focus of domestic HRM on issues of managing workforce diversity may prove to be beneficial to the practice of international HRM.

It is worthwhile examining in detail what is meant by the statement that international HRM is more complex than domestic HRM. Recently, Dowling[5] summarized the (rather sparse) literature on similarities and differences between international and domestic HRM. He concluded that the factors that differentiated international from domestic HRM were:

- ▸ More functions and activities
- ▸ Broader perspective
- ▸ More involvement in employees' personal lives
- ▸ Changes in emphasis as the workforce mix of PCNs and HCNs varies
- ▸ Risk exposure
- ▸ More external influences

Each of these factors will be discussed in some detail to illustrate the characteristics of each one.

More Functions and Activities

To operate in an international environment, a human resources department must engage in a number of activities that would not be necessary in a domestic environment: *international taxation, international relocation and orientation, administrative services for expatriates, host government relations,* and *language translation services.*

With regard to *international taxation,* expatriates typically have both domestic and host-country tax liabilities, so tax equalization policies must be designed to ensure that there is no tax incentive or disincentive associated with any particular international assignment.[6] The administration of tax equalization policies is complicated by the wide variations in tax laws across host countries and by the possible time lag between the completion of an expatriate assignment and the settlement of domestic and international tax liabilities. In recognition of these difficulties, most large international companies retain the services of a major accounting firm for international taxation advice.

International relocation and orientation involves arranging for predeparture training; providing immigration and travel details; providing housing, shopping, medical care, recreation, and schooling information; and finalizing compensation details such as delivery of salary overseas, determination of various overseas allowances, and taxation treatment. Many of these factors may be a source of anxiety for the expatriate and require considerable time and attention to successfully resolve potential problems — certainly much more time than would be involved in a domestic transfer/relocation.

An international company also needs to provide *administrative services* for expatriates in the host countries in which it operates. Commenting on the need for these services for expatriates, a consultant in the area of international HRM has noted that "anyone who has ever been responsible for an administrative service such as company-provided housing knows the importance of this activity, where both employees and spouses often 'help' the human resource manager by clarifying a policy and procedure."[7] Providing administrative services can often be a time-consuming and complex activity because policies and procedures are not always clear cut and may conflict with local conditions. For example, ethical questions can arise when a practice that is legal and accepted in the host country may be at best unethical and at worst illegal in the parent country. A situation may arise in which a host country requires an AIDS test for a work permit for an employee whose parent company is headquartered in California, where employment-related AIDS testing is illegal. How does the HR manager deal with the employee who refuses the assignment and the company that issues the assignment? These issues add to the complexity of providing administrative services to expatriates.

Host-government relations represent an important activity for an HR department, particularly in developing countries where work permits and other important certificates are often more easily obtained when a personal relationship exists between the relevant government officials and multinational company (MNC) managers. Maintaining such relationships helps resolve potential problems that can be caused by ambiguous eligibility and/or compliance criteria for documentation such as work permits. American MNCs, however, must be careful in how they deal with relevant government officials. Payment or payment-in-kind such as lunches, dinners, and gifts may violate the Foreign Corrupt Practices Act.

Provision of *language translation services* for internal and external personnel correspondence is an additional activity for an international HR department. Morgan[8] notes that if the HR department is the major user of language translation services, the role of this translation group is often expanded to provide translation services to all foreign operation departments within the company.

Broader Perspective

Domestic HR managers generally administer programs for a single national group of employees who are covered by a uniform compensation policy and taxed by a single government. Because international HR managers face the problem of designing and administering programs for more than one national group of employees (for example, PCN, HCN, and TCN employees who may work together at the regional headquarters of an overseas subsidiary), they need to take a more global view of issues. For example, a broader, more international perspective on expatriate benefits would endorse the view that all expatriate employees, regardless of nationality, should receive a foreign service or expatriate premium. Yet some international companies that routinely pay such premiums to their PCN employees on overseas assignment (even if the assignments are to desirable locations) do not pay premiums to foreign nationals assigned to the home country of the company. Such a policy confirms HCN and TCN employees' belief that PCN employees (expatriates) are given preferential treatment.[9] Complex equity issues arise when employees of various nationalities work together, and the resolution of these issues remains one of the major challenges in the international HRM field. (Equity issues with regard to compensation are discussed in Chapter 6.)

More Involvement in Employees' Lives

A greater degree of involvement in employees' personal lives is necessary for the selection, training, and effective management of expatriate employees and TCNs. The international HR department needs to ensure that the expatriate employee understands housing arrangements, health care, and all aspects of the compensation package provided for the assignment (cost-of-living allowances, premiums, taxes, and so on). Many international companies have an international personnel services branch that coordinates administration of the above programs and provides services for the expatriate employees and TCNs such as handling their banking, investments, and home rental while on assignment and coordinating home visits and final repatriation.

In the international setting, the HR department has much more direct contact with the employee's family than in a domestic setting. Typically, the HR department's involvement with an employee's family is limited to matters relating to company-provided insurance programs. Internationally, the HR department may need to help the family find adequate schooling and housing or, in remoter, less hospitable assignment locations, may be required to develop and even run recreational programs. For a domestic assignment, most of these matters either would not arise or would be primarily the responsibility of the employee rather than the HR department.

Changes in Emphasis as the Workforce
Mix of PCNs and HCNs Varies

As foreign operations mature, the emphases put on various human resource functions change. For example, as the need for expatriates declines and more trained HCNs become available, resources previously allocated to areas such as expatriate taxation, relocation, and orientation are transferred to activities such as HCN selection, training, and development. The last activity may require establishment of a program to bring high-potential HCNs to corporate headquarters for developmental assignments. This need to change emphasis in personnel operations as a foreign subsidiary matures is clearly a factor that would broaden the responsibilities of functions such as human resource planning, staffing, compensation, and training and development.

Risk Exposure

Frequently, the human and financial consequences of failure in the international arena are more severe than in domestic business. For example, expatriate failure (the premature return of an expatriate from an international assignment) is a persistent, high-cost problem for international companies.[10] Direct costs (salary, training costs, and travel and relocation expenses) per failure to the parent company may be as high as three times the domestic salary plus relocation expenses, depending on currency exchange rates and location of assignment.[11] Indirect costs such as loss of market share and damage to overseas customer relationships may be considerable.[12] The topic of expatriate failure rates is discussed in more detail in Chapter 3.

Another aspect of risk exposure that is relevant to international HRM is terrorism. Most major multinational companies must now consider this factor when planning international meetings and assignments. It is estimated that MNCs spend 1 to 2 percent of their revenues on protection against terrorism. Terrorism has also clearly had an effect on the way in which employees assess potential international assignment locations.[13]

More External Influences

The major external factors that influence international HRM are the type of government, the state of the economy, and the generally accepted practices of doing business in each of the various host countries in which the business enterprise operates. In developed countries, labor is more expensive and better organized than in less-developed countries, and governments require compliance with guidelines on issues such as labor relations, taxation, and health and safety. These factors shape the activities of the international HR manager to a considerable extent. In less-developed countries, labor tends to be cheaper and less organized, and government regulation is less pervasive, so these factors take less time. The HR manager must spend more time, however, learning and interpreting the local ways of doing business and the general code of conduct regarding activities such as bribery and gift giving. The HR manager may also become more involved in administering company-provided or -financed housing, education, and other facilities not readily available in the local economy.

VARIABLES THAT MODERATE DIFFERENCES BETWEEN DOMESTIC AND INTERNATIONAL HRM

In our discussion so far, we have argued that the complexity involved in operating in different countries and employing different national categories of employees is the main factor that differentiates domestic and international HRM, rather than any major differences between the HRM functions performed. In addition to complexity, there are two other variables that moderate (diminish or accentuate) differences between domestic and international HRM. These variables are the industry with which a company is involved and the attitudes of senior management.

Industry Type

Recent work by Porter[14] suggests that the industry (or industries if the organization is a conglomerate) in which a firm is involved is of considerable importance because patterns of international competition vary widely from one industry to another. At one end of the continuum of international competition is the *multidomestic industry*, one in which competition in each country is essentially independent of competition in other countries. Traditional examples include retailing, distribution, and insurance. The other end of the continuum is the *global industry*, one in which a firm's competitive position in one country is significantly influenced by its position in other countries. Examples include commercial aircraft, semiconductors, and copiers. The key distinction between a multidomestic industry and a global industry is described by Porter as follows:

> The global industry is not merely a collection of domestic industries but a series of linked domestic industries in which the rivals compete against each other on a truly worldwide basis. . . . In a multidomestic

11

industry, then, international strategy collapses to a series of domestic strategies. The issues that are uniquely international revolve around how to do business abroad, how to select good countries in which to compete (or assess country risk), and mechanisms to achieve the one-time transfer of know-how. These are questions that are relatively well-developed in the literature. In a global industry, however, managing international activities like a portfolio will undermine the possibility of achieving competitive advantage. In a global industry, a firm must in some way integrate its activities on a worldwide basis to capture the linkages among countries.

The important implications for the role of the HRM function in multidomestic and global industries can be analyzed using Porter's value-chain model[15] shown in Figure 1–2. In Porter's model, HRM is seen as one of four support activities for the five primary activities of the firm. Since human resources are involved in each of the primary and support activities, the HRM function is seen as cutting across the entire value chain of a firm. If the firm is in a multidomestic industry, the role of the HR department will most likely be more domestic in structure and orientation. At times there may be considerable demand for international services from the HRM function (for example, when a new plant or office is established in a foreign location and the need for expatriate employees arises), but these activities would not be pivotal — indeed, many of these services may be provided via consultants and/or temporary employees. The main role for the HRM function would be to support the primary activities of the firm in each domestic market to achieve a competitive advantage through either cost/efficiency or product/service differentiation.[16] If the firm is in a global industry, however, the "imperative for coordination" described by Porter would require a HRM function structured to deliver the international support required by the primary activities of the firm. The need to develop coordination raises complex problems for any international firm. As Laurent[17] has noted,

> In order to build, maintain, and develop their corporate identity, multinational organizations need to strive for consistency in their ways of managing people on a worldwide basis. Yet, and in order to be effective locally, they also need to adapt those ways to the specific cultural requirements of different societies. While the global nature of the business may call for increased consistency, the variety of cultural environments may be calling for differentiation.

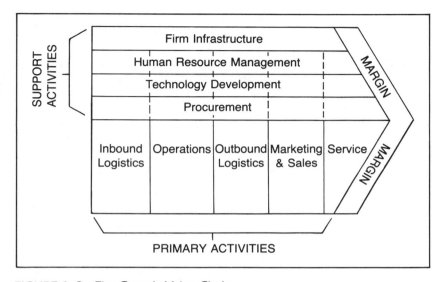

FIGURE 1-2 The Generic Value Chain
SOURCE: Reprinted with permission of The Free Press, a division of Macmillan, Inc. from *Competitive Advantage: Creating and Sustaining Superior Performance* by Michael E. Porter, p. 37. Copyright © 1985 by Michael E. Porter.

There is no easy solution to such a fundamental issue, and both Porter and Laurent recognize the complexities involved. In discussing possible solutions, Porter is the more circumspect and general: He notes that the ability to coordinate globally through the value chain is increasing because of modern technology, and he argues that a study of Japanese multinationals would be worthwhile, as "Japanese firms enjoy an organizational style that is supportive of coordination and a strong commitment to introducing new technologies such as information systems that facilitate it."[18]

Laurent is more specifically concerned with the HRM function and proposes that a truly international conception of human resource management would require the following steps:

1. An explicit recognition by the parent organization that its own peculiar ways of managing human resources reflect some assumptions and values of its home culture.

13

2. An explicit recognition by the parent organization that its peculiar ways are neither universally better nor worse than others but are different and likely to exhibit strengths and weaknesses, particularly abroad.

3. An explicit recognition by the parent organization that its foreign subsidiaries may have other preferred ways of managing people that are neither intrinsically better nor worse, but could possibly be more effective locally.

4. A willingness from headquarters to not only acknowledge cultural differences, but also to take active steps in order to make them discussable and therefore usable.

5. The building of a genuine belief by all parties involved that more creative and effective ways of managing people could be developed as a result of cross-cultural learning.

Laurent acknowledges that these are difficult steps that few organizations have taken: "They have more to do with states of mind and mindsets than with behaviors. As such, these processes can only be facilitated and this may represent a primary mission for executives in charge of international human resource management."[19]

Implicit in Laurent's analysis is the idea that by taking the steps he describes, an organization attempting to implement a global strategy via coordination of activities would be better able to work through the difficulties and complex trade-offs inherent in such a strategy. To date there is a dearth of research that investigates how organizations overcome the problems of coordination, but the ideas of Porter and Laurent are a valuable contribution to the emerging literature on the role of international HRM.

Attitudes of Senior Management to International Operations

The point made by Laurent that some of the changes required to truly internationalize the HR function "have more to do with states of mind and mindsets than with behaviors" illustrates the importance of a final variable that may moderate differences between international and domestic HRM: the attitudes of senior management to international operations.

It is likely that if senior management does not have a strong international orientation, the importance of international operations may be underemphasized (or possibly even ignored) in terms of corporate goals and objectives. In such situations, managers may tend to focus on domestic issues and minimize differences between international and domestic environments. They may assume that there is a great deal of transferability between domestic and international HRM practices. This failure to recognize differences in managing human resources in foreign environments — regardless of whether it is because of ethnocentrism, inadequate information, or a lack of international perspective — frequently results in major difficulties in international operations.[20] It is becoming increasingly apparent that such a domestic orientation is dysfunctional for many companies. Professor Christopher Bartlett of the Harvard Business School argues that "competitiveness is already beyond the reach of the purely national company. New products are getting costlier and harder to develop, and shorter life cycles mean that companies have to develop them and get them to global markets faster than ever."[21] According to Wharton professor Stephen Kobrin, "Even the biggest companies in the biggest markets cannot survive on their domestic markets if they are in global industries. They have to be in all major markets. That means North America, Western Europe, and the Pacific Rim countries."[22] This is not to say that every company in every industry has to be a global player, but thinking globally is likely to enhance an organization's ability to survive and adapt in the twenty-first century.

SUMMARY

The purpose of this chapter has been to provide an overview of the field of international HRM. We did this by discussing a model and definition of international HRM and examining how this differed from domestic HRM. We concluded that the complexity involved in operating in different countries and employing different national categories of employees is the main factor differentiating domestic and international HRM, rather than any major differences between the HRM functions performed. This complexity may be moderated by the nature of the industry structure in which the company is engaged (for example, global vs. multidomestic) and the attitudes of senior management in the company to international operations.

In our discussion of the international dimensions of HRM in this book, we shall be drawing on the HRM literature. Subsequent chapters will examine the international dimensions of the major functional areas of HRM: human resource planning, recruitment and selection, performance evaluation, compensation, training and development, and labor relations. We will provide comparative data on HRM practices in different countries, but our major emphasis is on the international dimensions of HRM confronting MNCs, particularly those dealing with expatriate employees.[23]

QUESTIONS

1. What are the main similarities and differences between domestic and international HRM?
2. Define these terms: PCN, HCN, and TCN.
3. Discuss two HR activities in which an MNC must engage that would not be required in a domestic environment.
4. Why is a greater degree of involvement in employees' personal lives inevitable in many international HRM activities?
5. Discuss the variables that moderate differences between domestic and international HR practices.

FURTHER READING

1. P. J. Dowling, "Human Resource Issues in International Business," *Syracuse Journal of International Law and Commerce*, Vol. 13, No. 2 (1986) pp. 255–271.
2. ———. "International HRM," in *Human Resource Management: Evolving Roles and Responsibilities*, Volume 1, ed. L. Dyer. ASPA/BNA Handbook of Human Resource Management series. Washington, D.C.: BNA, 1988.
3. *Human Resource Management*, Vol. 25, No. 1 (1986). Symposium on international human resource management issue.
4. *Human Resource Management*, Vol. 27, No. 1 (1988). Symposium on human resource management in the multinational corporation issue.
5. J. Main, "B-Schools Get a Global Vision," *Fortune*, July 17, 1989, pp. 78–86.
6. C. Vance and M. Sailer, "Human Resource Management Issues in Europe," in *Readings and Cases in International Human Resource Management*, ed. M. Mendenhall and G. Oddou (Boston: PWS-KENT Publishing Co., 1991).

NOTES

1. "The New Shape of Global Business," *Fortune*, July 31, 1989, pp. 280–323.

2. M. G. Duerr, "International Business Management: Its Four Tasks," *Conference Board Record*, October 1986, p. 43.

3. P. V. Morgan, "International Human Resource Management: Fact or Fiction," *Personnel Administrator*, Vol. 31, No. 9 (1986) pp. 43–47.

4. R. L. Desatnick and M. L. Bennett, *Human Resource Management in the Multinational Company* (New York: Nichols, 1978).

5. P. J. Dowling, "International and Domestic Personnel/Human Resource Management: Similarities and Differences," in *Readings in Personnel and Human Resource Management* (3rd ed.), ed. R. S. Schuler, S. A. Youngblood, and V. L. Huber (St. Paul, Minn.: West Publishing Co., 1988).

6. See D. L. Pinney, "Structuring an Expatriate Tax Reimbursement Program," *Personnel Administrator*, Vol. 27, No. 7 (1982) pp. 19–25; and M. Gajek and M. M. Sabo, "The Bottom Line: What HR Managers Need to Know About the New Expatriate Regulations," *Personnel Administrator*, Vol. 31, No. 2 (1986) pp. 87–92.

7. F. Acuff, "International and Domestic Human Resources Functions," in Organization Resources Counselors, *Innovations in International Compensation* (New York, 1984).

8. Morgan, "International Human Resource Management."

9. R. D. Robinson, *International Business Management: A Guide to Decision Making*, 2nd. ed. (Hinsdale, Ill.: Dryden, 1978).

10. R. L. Tung, "Selection and Training of Personnel for Overseas Assignments," *Columbia Journal of World Business*, Vol. 16, No. 1 (1981) pp. 68–78.

11. M. Mendenhall and G. Oddou, "The Dimensions of Expatriate Acculturation: A Review," *Academy of Management Review*, Vol. 10 (1985) pp. 39–47; M. G. Harvey, "The Multinational Corporation's Expatriate Problem: An Application of Murphy's Law," *Business Horizons*, Vol. 26, No. 1 (1983) pp. 71–78.

12. Y. Zeira and M. Banai, "Present and Desired Methods of Selecting Expatriate Managers for International Assignments," *Personnel Review*, Vol. 13, No. 3 (1984) pp. 29–35.

13. "How U.S. Executives Dodge Terrorism Abroad," *Business Week*, May 12, 1986, p. 41; and "Terrorism," Chapter 4 in T. M. Gladwin and I. Walter, *Multinationals Under Fire: Lessons in the Management of Conflict* (New York: John Wiley, 1980).

14. M. E. Porter, "Changing Patterns of International Competition," *California Management Review*, Vol. 28, No. 2 (1986) pp. 9–40.

15. M. E. Porter, *Competitive Advantage: Creating and Sustaining Superior Performance* (New York: The Free Press, 1985).

16. See R. S. Schuler, and I. C. MacMillan, "Gaining Competitive Advantage Through Human Resource Management Practices," *Human Resource Management*, Vol. 23, No. 3 (1984) pp. 241–255, for a discussion of these strategies.

17. A. Laurent, "The Cross-Cultural Puzzle of International Human Resource Management," *Human Resource Management*, Vol. 25 (1986) pp. 91–102.

18. Porter, "Changing Patterns," p. 37.

19. Laurent, "The Cross-Cultural Puzzle," p. 100.

20. Desatnick and Bennett, *Human Resource Management in the Multinational Company.*

21. *Fortune*, March 14, 1986, p. 18; A. Bennett, "Going Global: The Chief Executive in the Year 2000 Will Be Experienced Abroad," *Wall Street Journal*, February 27, 1989; and L. Bruce, "Wanted: More Mongrels in the Corporate Kennel," *International Management*, January 1989, pp. 35–37. *Note:* Rosalie Tung and Ed Miller are currently conducting research regarding succession planning in MNCs. Ed Miller told us (August 22, 1989) that 93 percent of the U.S. firms they sampled indicated that an international assignment was not important at all as a criterion for advancement to the senior management level.

22. J. Main, "How to Go Global and Why," *Fortune*, August 28, 1989, p. 70.

23. For an excellent example of a comparative HRM study, see N. K. Napier and R. B. Peterson, *An International Perspective on Personnel Management* (Neutral Bay Junction, Australia: World Federation of Personnel Management Associations, 1989).

CHAPTER 2

▼

Strategic Corporate Planning and International HRM Planning

▲

International human resource management allows corporate strategists to plan for the human resource needs of the MNC. Effective planning depends on a knowledge of the relationships between corporate strategy, organizational structure, and human resource practices, as "the fundamental strategic management problem is to keep the strategy, structure and human resource dimensions of the organization in direct alignment."[1] Consequently, these factors are the central topics of this chapter. First, MNC strategy and structure variations are described. Next, the implications for international human resource practices are drawn out. Finally, the potential matches and choices among strategy, structure, and HRM philosophies are discussed. This discussion illustrates the extensive relationship between strategic corporate planning and international human resource planning.

MNC STRATEGY AND STRUCTURE

Any multinational firm's strategy and structure influences and is influenced by international human resource management practices. To understand these various practices, it is necessary to understand first the choices MNCs have when deciding on their overall structure and strategy. The organizational strategy and structure define the tasks of individuals and business units within the firm and the processes that result from the intertwined tasks. They also identify how the organization is divided up (differentiated) and how it is united (integrated). Ultimately, the effectiveness of the individuals and units and, therefore, the survival of the firm are influenced by its structure and strategy.

Another variable influencing strategy and structure is the growth and development of the organization.[2] Most MNCs traditionally pass through several stages of organizational development as the nature and size of their international activities alter. As they go through these evolutionary stages, their organizational structures change. Typically, the strain imposed by the spread into new foreign markets threatens the organizational structure. Thus, growth, coupled with international environmental factors (such as host-government regulations regarding equity and labor) and the need for coordination across business units, influences the strategy/structure response.

A decision to move into a different development stage, although not always rational or methodical, can be regarded as a decision of strategy. The choice of structure evolves to correspond with the changes in the MNC's strategy.[3] Decisions regarding HRM practices generally emerge as a result of these two decisions. Therefore, the MNC's strategy and structure have significant implications for international human resource management. As human resource management effectiveness depends on its fit with the MNC's stage of development,[4] it is important to examine the path a multinational firm takes as it grows and develops and the HRM responses required at each stage.

STAGES OF INTERNATIONALIZATION

The evolution from a domestic to a truly global organization generally involves several stages. The number of stages varies from firm to firm, as does the time frame. Some companies go through the various stages rapidly while others evolve slowly over many years.[5] Not all firms internationalize in a sequential manner through the various stages, as many enter via acquisitions, thus leapfrogging into the internationalization process.[6] As we have said, linked to this evolutionary process are structural responses, control mechanisms, and HRM policies, as Exhibit 2–1 shows. The following analysis highlights these linkages by examining the typical path from domestic to global organization.

Stage 1: Export

This initial stage rarely involves much organizational response until the level of export sales reaches a critical point. Exporting tends to be handled by a middle person (for example, an export agent or foreign distributor). As export sales increase, an export manager may be appointed to control foreign sales and actively seek new markets. Further growth in exporting usually sees the establishment of an export department at the same level as the domestic sales department. This reflects a major commitment to the export activity.[7] At this stage, domestic staff are utilized to control exporting from the domestic-based home office, with the export manager paying frequent visits to the foreign markets. The HRM department (if one formally exists) handles any administrative, selection, and compensation tasks as an adjunct to the domestic activities.

Stage 2: Sales Subsidiary

As the organization develops expertise in foreign markets, agents and distributors are replaced by direct sales with the establishment of sales subsidiaries or branch offices in the foreign market countries. This stage may be prompted by problems with foreign agents, more confidence in the international sales activity, the desire to have greater control, and/or the decision to give greater support to the exporting activity, usually due to its increasing importance to the overall success of the organization. At this point, the organization must make a decision regarding staffing. If it wishes to maintain control of the sales subsidiary, it usually opts to staff the subsidiary from its headquarters (PCNs). If it regards country-specific factors — knowledge of the foreign market, language, sensitivity to host-country needs, and so on—as important, it may staff the subsidiary with host-country nationals (HCNs).

If the organization decides to use PCNs, the role of the corporate HRM department is limited to supervising the selection and compensation of staff for the export department and sales subsidiary. As Exhibit 2–1 shows, most firms opt for HCNs at this stage.

EXHIBIT 2-1 Evolution and Growth of International Business and Corresponding Changes

Evolution and growth of international business	A. Evolution of organizational structure	B. Other structural characteristics	C. Ownership policies	D. Control strategies	E. Staffing policies
I. Initial stage	Export dept.	Loose, formal relationships	Minority HQ* equity	Indirect, loose coupling	Host-country national in charge
II. Early production stage	Export dept./international division	More formalized relationships between HQ* and sub†	Minority or 50–50 equity	Indirect control through technical personnel	Home-country nationals in charge
III. Standardization of production process—mature stage; few products	International division	Increased formalized relationships	Majority or 100% equity in subsidiary operation	Direct control, tight coupling	Host country nationals in charge
IV. Product innovations and growth through diversification	Product/area bases for structuring of organization	Increased formalization	Minority or 50–50 equity	Indirect control through personnel	Home country or third country nationals in charge
V. Quest for global rationalization	Product/area bases for structuring matrix type organization	Increased formalization	Majority or 100% equity in subsidiary	Direct control	Host country nationals in charge

*HQ: Headquarters   †Sub: Subsidiaries

SOURCE: A. R. Negandhi, *International Management* (Boston: Allyn & Bacon, 1987), p. 23.

Stage 3: International Division

For some firms, it is a short step from the establishment of a sales subsidiary to foreign production. This step may be considered small if the firm is already assembling the product abroad (to take advantage of cheap labor or to save shipping costs or tariffs, for example). Alternatively, the firm may have a well-established export and marketing program that enables it to take advantage of host-government incentives or counter host-government controls on foreign imports by establishing a foreign production facility. Other firms find the transition to foreign investment a large, sometimes prohibitive, step. For example, an Australian firm that was successfully exporting mining equipment to Canada began to experience problems with after-sales servicing and delivery schedules. The establishment of its own production facility was considered too great a step, so the firm entered into a licensing agreement with a Canadian manufacturer.[8]

The structural response to foreign production tends to be the creation of a separate international division in which all international activities are grouped (see Figure 2–1) and managed by a senior executive at the corporate headquarters.[9] Most organizations at this stage of internationalization place great emphasis on control mechanisms and staff the foreign facility with PCNs, particularly as the organization expands its foreign production activities into several countries.

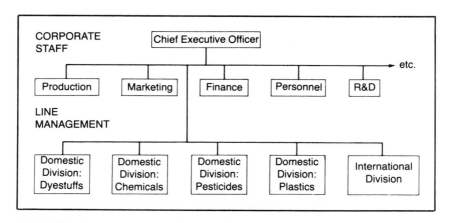

FIGURE 2–1 International Division Structure
SOURCE: A. V. Phatak, *International Dimensions of Management*, 2nd ed. (Boston: PWS-KENT Publishing Co., 1989), p. 84.

We should point out here that most U.S. manufacturing firms stumbled into manufacturing abroad without much design. Conscious strategies for growth on a global scale emerged later. Early investments in foreign production facilities were often defensive reactions against the threat of losing markets that in the first place had been acquired almost accidentally.[10] The structure and control mechanisms of early foreign production reflect this step into becoming a multinational without having had an explicit plan for doing so.[11] Consequently, the international division is typically considered an independent part of the enterprise and not subject to the same strategic planning that guides domestic activities.[12] At this stage, the international HRM activity is primarily concerned with PCN management, selection, and compensation. The emphasis is on identifying employees who can direct the daily operations of the foreign subsidiaries, supervising transfer of managerial and technical know-how, communicating corporate policies, and keeping corporate HQ informed.[13]

European MNCs have tended to take a different structural path than U.S. MNCs. Franko's study of seventy European MNCs revealed that European firms moved directly from a functional "mother-daughter" structure to a divisionalized global structure (with worldwide product or area divisions) or matrix organization without the transitional stage of an international division.[14] Human resource management practices, changing to serve the needs of the new structure, adjusted accordingly. Swedish MNCs have traditionally adopted the mother-daughter structure, but research by Hedlund[15] reveals that this is changing. These MNCs tend to adopt a mixture of elements of the mother-daughter structure and elements of the product division.

Japanese MNCs are evolving along similar lines to their U.S. counterparts. Export divisions have become international divisions but, according to Ronen,[16] the rate of change is slower. The characteristics of Japanese organizational culture (such as the control and reporting mechanisms and decision-making systems), the role of trading companies, and the systems of management appear to contribute to the slow evolution of the international division. These characteristics also inhibit the transition to the next stage of internationalization.

Stage 4: Global Product/Area Division

At this point, the organization is moving from the early foreign production stage into a phase of growth through production standardization and diversification. In the process, the international division becomes overstretched. The strain of sheer size can create problems of effective communication and efficiency of operation. Typically, tensions stem from the need for national responsiveness at the subsidiary unit and global integration at the parent headquarters. The demand for national responsiveness at the subsidiary unit develops because of factors such as differences in market structures, distribution channels, customer needs, local culture, and pressure from the host government. The need for more centralized global integration by the headquarters comes from having multinational customers, global competitors, and increasingly rapid flow of information and technology and from needing large volume for economies of scale. Resulting from this situation is the need for MNCs to grapple with two major issues of structure:

- ▸ the extent or degree to which key decisions are to be made at parent headquarters or at the subsidiary units (centralization vs. decentralization), and
- ▸ the type or form of control exerted by the parent over the subsidiary unit.[17]

The structural response can be either a product-based global structure (if the growth strategy is through product diversification) or an area-based structure (if the growth strategy is through geographical expansion); see Figure 2–2.[18] One could say that, by this stage, the organization has "come of age" as a multinational. Strategic planning now is carried out on a consistent and worldwide basis (though not all MNCs are equally successful in doing so). This stage marks the really decisive point in the transition to global organization: Top managers recognize that strategic planning and major policy decisions must be made in the central HQ so that a worldwide perspective on the interests of the total enterprise can be maintained.[19]

This transformation into a full-fledged multinational not only changes the focus of the HRM international activities, but alters the organization of the HRM function as well.[20] As we have seen, at the international division stage the international HRM policies are designed primarily to fit the domestic operations. Gradually, as the MNC strives to adapt its HRM activities to each host country's specific requirements, the HRM function changes. The PCN workforce remains under the control of the corporate HRM department, but local employees become the responsibility of each subsidiary. Corporate HRM staff perform a monitoring role and intervene in local affairs only in extreme circumstances. For example, Ford Australia has a ceiling on its HRM decisions, and those that involve an amount above that ceiling must be referred to

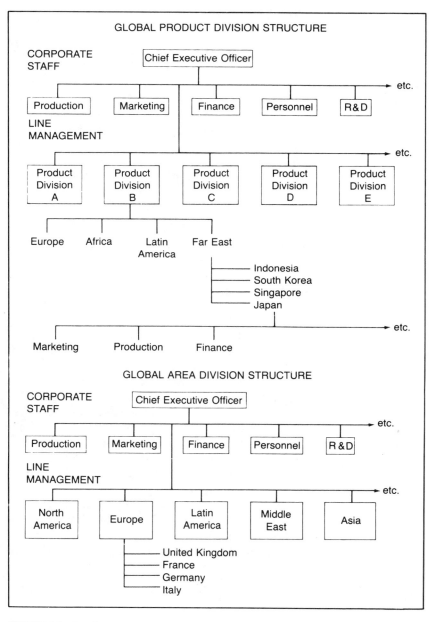

FIGURE 2-2 Global Product and Global Area Division Structures
SOURCE: A. V. Phatak, *International Dimensions of Management*, 2nd ed. (Boston: PWS-KENT Publishing Co., 1989), p. 90, p. 93.

regional HQ for corporate approval. This HRM monitoring role reflects management's desire for central control of strategic planning.

The HRM planning process becomes more complex as the organization develops. The coordination of activities and the formation of strategies for worldwide markets develop into independent managerial functions requiring specialized expertise. The growth in foreign exposure combined with changes in the organizational structure of international operations results in an increase in the number of managerial-class employees needed to oversee the contracts between the parent firm and its foreign affiliates. Within the human resource function, the development of managers able to operate in international environments becomes a new imperative.[21]

Stage 5: Global Multidimensional

The trend toward a global perspective accelerates as the MNC grows and is compounded by the complex international environment. Forces from global competitors, global customers, universal products, technological investments, and world-scale factories push the MNC toward global integration while host governments push for local responsiveness. The response has been a move to a matrix or mixed structure, as shown in Figure 2–3.[22]

In the matrix structure, the international or geographical division and the product division share joint authority. This type of organization violates Fayol's principle of unity of command and brings into the management system a philosophy of matching the structure to the decision-making process. Conflicts of interest are brought out into the open, and each issue that has priority in the decision making has an executive champion to ensure it is not neglected. Therefore, managers with functional, geographical, and product group responsibilities have similar status to those in foreign subsidiaries. Here, the MNC is attempting to integrate its operations across more than one dimension.

Popular in the early 1970s, the matrix structure has declined. It was an expensive method of organization that required careful implementation and commitment on the part of top management to be successful. Galbraith and Kazanjian[23] argue that the matrix "continues to be the only organizational form which fits the strategy of simultaneous pursuit of multiple business dimensions, with each given equal priority. . . . [T]he structural form succeeds because it fits the situation. Thus matrix can work when it evolves, not when it is installed." They also cite ex-

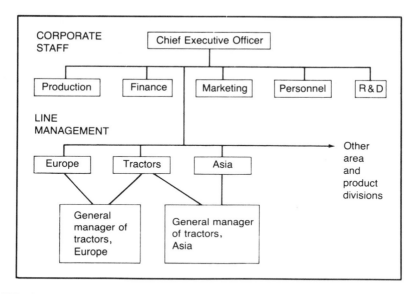

FIGURE 2-3 The Matrix Structure
SOURCE: A. V. Phatak, *International Dimensions of Management*, 2nd. ed. (Boston: PWS-KENT Publishing Co., 1989), p. 100.

amples of matrix-like or mixed structures that emerged in response to global pressures and trade-offs:

> For example, organizations that pursued area structures kept these geographical profit centers, but added worldwide product managers. Colgate-Palmolive has always had strong country managers. But, as they doubled the funding for product research, and as Colgate Dental Creme became a universal product, product managers were added at the corporate office to direct the R & D funding and coordinate marketing programs worldwide.
>
> Similarly, the product-divisionalized firms have been reintroducing the international division. At Motorola, the product groups had worldwide responsibility for their product lines. As they compete with the Japanese in Japan, an international group has been introduced to help coordinate across product lines.[24]

At this stage the MNC is grappling with a complex environment, global competition, strategy integration, and control. The structural responses attempt to coordinate global activities, so it is worthwhile to pause here and examine the centralization-decentralization issue and related control mechanisms.

Centralization vs. Decentralization

The degree of centralization is influenced by such factors as subsidiary size, market growth, parent nationality, parent wishes, and subsidiary-country conditions.[25] Research is mixed on the impact of subsidiary size. Some research suggests that the MNC will use a centralized structure for subsidiaries that represent a large percentage (over 50 percent, for example) of total firm sales. Other research, however, suggests the reverse: As foreign subsidiaries grow larger, the structure is less centralized because the parent would otherwise be overloaded by too many decisions and because subsidiaries may be less dependent on parent resources.

In MNCs in which the subsidiaries operate in high-growth markets with global competition, MNCs often seek broader perspectives and thus use more centralized structures. Firm nationality has also been found to affect structure. West European and Japanese firms, for example, tend to be more centralized than American-owned firms. There can also be subjective reasons for a given structure; for example, parent management may want to retain power.

In addition, decisions regarding structure often stem from demands at the subsidiary or host-country level. For instance, decentralized structures are more common when subsidiaries are less dependent on the parent for resources such as management talent, technology, and marketing expertise. If the subsidiary moves into businesses outside the MNC core business area and parent management is unable to understand those new areas, it will decentralize decision making. When the host government demands more input or requires joint ventures, decentralization of decision making may be necessary. Expertise in human resource management (and other areas) is more likely to be transferred under a centralized structure, as the MNC and subsidiary have a much closer relationship and greater frequency of information transfer than under a decentralized structure.

The MNC does not have to choose between centralization and decentralization. Instead, it can take a combination of approaches, depending on environmental changes (such as host-government policy changes) or organizational development. Many MNCs centralize management decisions such as R & D and finance while decentralizing functions such as marketing and personnel. The rule of thumb seems to be to centralize strategic areas and decentralize operational issues.

Control

In addition to the degree of centralization, the choice of control systems may affect the type and degree of integration. Two major types of control have been identified: output-oriented and culture-oriented systems. The output-oriented control systems involve monitoring through objective data. Subsidiaries typically provide data on performance measures, financial information, plans, and budgets. For example, IBM requires all operating units to provide data on the same thirteen performance elements, including both quantitative (e.g., cost/revenue mix and business volume) and qualitative (e.g., manpower status) outputs.

The culture-oriented control systems tend to be behavioral and subtle. These control systems rely on social interaction, personnel transfers, and socialization of employees to direct and control subsidiary performance. Such control encourages subsidiary members to acquire and develop the company-wide understanding of appropriate behavior and goals. This is sometimes achieved by sending PCNs to subsidiaries to exchange and transfer expertise and information and to train and socialize new organization members.

Firms may use composite control approaches, including both output and culture controls. In output control systems, MNCs are likely to transfer people with technical skills. In cultural-oriented control systems, headquarters managers transferred to subsidiaries bring knowledge about the firm's culture, which is seen as part of its competitive advantage. Thus global MNC organizations use an "integrated network" of tight output controls and a shared strategic process, coupled with heavy flows and transfers of technical, financial, and other staff between parent and subsidiary, to instill the firm's culture and transfer expertise. In so doing they enter into another phase of development sometimes referred to as the transnational state. As Pucik[26] states:

> The evolution of the multinational human resource function does not come to an end, even after the selection, reward, appraisal and development systems are firmly established on the operational and managerial levels. The continuous globalization of corporate business activities together with an increased complexity of the underlying

organizational structure may require corresponding adjustment of the human resource system to the more strategically-oriented perspective.

If the MNC chooses to exert, integrate, and control by cultural and subjective means, a geocentric approach to human resource management practices may be taken. (This approach is discussed later in this chapter.) International assignments become an essential element of executive training and development for the large MNCs with substantial investments abroad. Such foreign assignments are essential in the evolution of a truly multinational perspective.[27]

The above discussion highlights the increased demands for the international HRM function. If the MNC opts for a matrix organization, particular care must be taken with staffing. As Ronen[28] notes:

> It requires managers who know the business in general, who have good interpersonal skills, and who can deal with the ambiguities of responsibility and authority inherent in the matrix system. Training in such skills as planning procedures, the kinds of interpersonal skills necessary for the matrix, and the kind of analysis and orderly presentation of ideas essential to planning within a group is most important for supporting the matrix approach. Moreover, management development and human resource planning are even more necessary in the volatile environment of the matrix than in the traditional organizations.

Although each of these stages of international business development is complex to manage effectively, many firms face even more complexity due to mixed forms of structure. In a recent survey conducted by Dowling,[29] more than one-third of the firms indicated that they had mixed forms. Of all the firms with international operations, the types of structures represented included:

▸ International operations organized into national subsidiaries   11.8%
  with local coordination of production/services, marketing, personnel, etc.

▸ International division structure with senior management re-   14.7%
  porting to president or CEO of company.

▸ One or more regional headquarters used to coordinate pro-   20.6%
  duction/services, marketing, and personnel among national operations.

▸ World-product or world-matrix structure used for coordina-   17.6%
tion of international operations.

▸ Mixed forms of structure.   35.3%

Stage 6: The Transnational

Some writers are identifying a new stage of organization development that builds on the global product/area and matrix structures. It is characterized by an interdependence of resources and responsibilities across all business units regardless of national boundaries. In addition, a set of strong cross-unit integrating devices, a strong corporate identity, and a well-developed worldwide management perspective are present. The term *transnational* has been coined to describe this new form. In a recent study Bartlett and Ghoshal[30] noted:

> Among the companies we studied, there were several that were in the process of developing such organizational capabilities. They had surpassed the classic capabilities of the *multinational* company that operates as decentralized federations of units able to sense and respond to diverse international needs and opportunities; and they had evolved beyond the abilities of the global company with its facility for managing operations on a tightly controlled worldwide basis through its centralized hub structure. They had developed what we termed *transnational* capabilities — the ability to manage across national boundaries, retaining local flexibility while achieving global integration. More than anything else this involved the ability to link local operations to each other and to the center in a flexible way, and in so doing, to leverage those local and central capabilities.

Multinationals that develop transnational capabilities inevitably take jobs away from some locations and run afoul of the "good citizen" commitment. Nevertheless, economic realities are forcing them to become transnational systems. The political world in which every business has to operate is becoming more nationalistic and more protectionist — indeed, more chauvinistic—day by day in every major country, but the multinational has little choice. If it fails to adjust to transnational economic reality, it will fast become inefficient and uneconomical — a bureaucratic "cost center" rather than a "profit center." It must succeed in becoming a bridge between both the realities of a rapidly integrating world economy and a splintering world polity.[31]

As a corporate business becomes more and more transnational, the resulting complexity embedded in the multilayer matrix structure often becomes an obstacle to efficient communication and decision making. Under such conditions, the time is ripe to move away from a formal matrix structure as the key coordination and control tool. Supporting a climate in which matrix-like behavior is a natural pattern of action on operational, managerial, and strategic levels becomes the new task facing the transnational human resource system. Even when corporate businesses are restricted to a relatively limited geographic area, it is not easy to manage effectively the transition from a formal matrix structure to an informal matrix culture.[32]

The needs of global business in the 1990s require careful monitoring of conditions in the global environment and planning of competitive strategies well in advance. This monitoring and planning in turn requires the creation and maintenance of a corporate executive cadre able to monitor global markets, respond rapidly to emerging global opportunities and threats, and formulate and execute the appropriate long-term business strategies in the global context. Thus, the emerging demand for managers of global strategies cannot be met without a further strengthening of strategic human resource activities in the corporation and their adaptation to the contingencies of transnational operations.

OTHER FACTORS IN MNC STRATEGY

Cooperative Ventures/Strategic Partnerships

To add to the complexities of MNC management and HRM planning, some MNCs enter into various types of cooperative ventures or strategic partnerships, which add another dimension to the strategy-structure mix. Lorange classified four types of cooperative ventures: (1) project based, (2) licensing, (3) those with permanent complementary roles, and (4) joint ownership.[33] A particular type of venture emerges as a function of the strategic importance of the venture to the parent company and the extent to which the parent seeks control over the resources allocated to the venture.

An example of a cooperative venture as a strategic response is that of Philips, which has expanded its use of strategic partnering in order to deal with the realities of the communications industry:

> An important strategy is to extend our strength in the widening arena of action by strategic partnering. Although our involvement in co-

operative activity dates back to the thirties, we have intensively accelerated these partnerships in recent years with acquisitions, joint ventures, license contracts, and othe forms of cooperation. We have pursued these arrangements in almost every area of technology that falls within our scope: audio, video, lighting, telephone, domestic appliances, optical data storage, optical fibers, and integrated circuits.[34]

These cooperative activities were entered into by Philips for a variety of reasons:

- ▸ to achieve economies of scale
- ▸ to share the costs and risks of R & D
- ▸ to achieve product standardization in order to produce global products
- ▸ to strengthen product activities in which Philips is already involved

Similar activities are occurring in the automobile, aerospace, computer, and biotechnology industries. For some organizations, cooperative ventures are the only method of entry into some markets, and the joint venture partner is the host government.

For each of the four types of cooperative ventures, Lorange suggests there are several human resource policy issues: (1) assignment of executives, (2) evaluation and promotion of managers, (3) the type of control systems used, (4) loyalty of managers to the venture or to their respective parents, and (5) expected time for managers to spend on strategic versus operational issues.[35] These issues need to be resolved by MNCs, but Shenkar and Zeira have indicated that there is a lack of research to guide a discussion or offer a prescription.[36] They have, however, offered a model to help identify various human resource problems and concerns in international ventures. They have suggested that characteristics of the parent (composition of the workforce, source of employees, and so on), system characteristics of the firm (for example, strategy and differentiation), and structural characteristics of the firm (such as size) affect the number and types of employee groups for the venture and the managerial and personnel processes to use with employees.

Fashion or Fit?

The above discussion has traced the evolution of the organization from a domestic-oriented to a global-oriented firm. A note of caution should be added. Growth in the firm's international business activity does require structural responses, but the evolutionary process will differ across MNCs. As pointed out earlier, U.S., European, Swedish, and Japanese MNCs have different structural responses to growth. Other variables — size of organization, pattern of internationalization, management policies, and so on — also play a part in the strategy-structure mix. Researchers have identified the pattern described here, but the danger is to treat the stages as normative rather than descriptive. To quote Bartlett:[37]

> For some MNCs it seemed that organizational structure followed fashion as much as it related to strategy. Reorganizations from international divisions to global product or area organizations, or from global structures to matrix forms, became widespread. This, after all, was the classic organizational sequence described in the "stages theories."
>
> Yet many companies that had expected such changes to provide them with the strategy-structure "fit" to meet the new pressures were disappointed. Developing a multidimensional decision-making process that was able to balance the conflicting global and national needs was a subtle and time-consuming process not necessarily achieved by redrawing the lines on a chart. Examples of failed or abandoned multinational organizations abound.

It is also important to remember that strategy and structure influence international HRM planning and policy. For this reason, we have tried to draw out the HRM implications at each stage of the organization's development. The role of HRM is crucial, as the ability to develop a flexible global organization that is centrally integrated and coordinated yet locally responsive requires effective strategic management. Therefore, the MNC must have appropriate HRM policies for staff selection, performance appraisal, rewards, and training that will enhance its overall performance and competitive advantage strategies. Human resource managers should be involved directly in the formulation of strategy as well as in the implementation of that strategy. The rest of this chapter addresses this international HRM planning role.

INTERNATIONAL HUMAN RESOURCE MANAGEMENT APPROACHES

The HRM literature uses four terms to describe MNC approaches to managing and staffing their subsidiaries, and these approaches are determined to a large extent by the attitudes of top management at headquarters and the strategy-structure mix. Although these approaches will be examined in detail in the next chapter, it is important to define them here, as they have a bearing on international HRM strategy. The four approaches are:[38]

1. *Ethnocentric:* Few foreign subsidiaries have any autonomy, strategic decisions are made at headquarters, and key jobs at both domestic and foreign operations are held by headquarters management personnel. Subsidiaries, in other words, are managed by expatriates from the home country (PCNs).

2. *Polycentric:* The MNC treats each subsidiary as a distinct national entity with some decision-making autonomy. Subsidiaries are usually managed by local nationals (HCNs) who are seldom promoted to positions at headquarters.

3. *Regiocentric:* Reflects the geographic strategy and structure of the MNC. Like the geocentric approach, it utilizes a wider pool of managers but in a limited way (personnel may move outside their countries but only within the particular geographic region). Regional managers may not be promoted to headquarters positions but enjoy a degree of regional autonomy in decision making.

4. *Geocentric:* The organization ignores nationality in favor of ability. This approach to staffing without regard to nationality must be accompanied by a worldwide integrated business strategy to be successful.

Exhibit 2–2 summarizes these four approaches and illustrates their impact on aspects of the MNC.

Which approach should be used when developing a strategy for international HRM? The answer — "it all depends!" — should come as no surprise. Factors such as strategy, structure, size, availability of staff, headquarters attitudes, and government regulations determine the approach. As Evans states:[39]

> The choice of a global geocentric or polycentric approach to human resource management is not dictated by product-market or industry logic; each approach represents a different way of coping with the different socio-cultural environments of a multinational company. . . . Thus firms in worldwide industries where divisions and subsidiaries are interdependent would be advised to adopt global human resource strategies: the costs of such strategies would be outweighed by the potentially enormous returns of a successful global strategy. Firms where divisions and business elements can be discreetly and independently defined would be advised to adopt cheaper polycentric human resource strategies. Some of the disadvantages of either ex-

treme position can be counteracted by the use of subtle management processes.

Organizational structure and strategy influence the approach to international HRM. For example, the global firm manages its global workforce in a centralized or at least coordinated way. Corporate policy on human resource management is relatively specific and influential. There are numerous guidelines, policies, principles, and guiding corporate values; desired personnel practices are often prescribed. Specific examples are worldwide policies on open-door grievance procedure, single status, and stance toward unions; a uniform procedure of performance evaluation or global compensation policies; monitoring of human resource management through opinion surveys that compare the performance of business units and divisions; and a code of corporate values that guide the indoctrination of new recruits. International transfers of staff are used for management development and socialization to foster commitment to the global organization. Well-known global enterprises include IBM, Hewlett-Packard, Procter & Gamble, Shell, and Unilever.

The polycentric firm, on the other hand, decentralizes the management of human resources to the level of business operations in each foreign country location. Corporate coordination, if it exists, is loose and informal. There are few corporate guidelines, vague policies, and no specification of desired practice. All this is left to the foreign subsidiary's general manager and his or her personnel staff, who adapt not only to local product-market conditions but also to local sociocultural circumstances. The role of the headquarters staff is limited to high-potential identification and development (ensuring a supply of appropriate general managers to run decentralized companies) and the organization of occasional meetings of subsidiary executives to exchange the lessons of experience. Examples of polycentric enterprises are Schlumberger, Holderbank (the Swiss enterprise that is the world leader in the cement industry), American Express, GEC in Britain, the Swedish gas firm AGA, and Nestlé.[40]

The ethnocentric firm tends to be at the early stages of internationalization. Because the firm needs to tightly control its foreign business activity, it relies on the use of expatriate managers and technical staff to transfer operational and reporting systems. Once the foreign subsidiary is well established, the expatriates may be replaced by HCNs.

The regiocentric firm falls between the ethnocentric and polycentric approaches. It provides control to its managers, but the control is

EXHIBIT 2-2 Four Types of Headquarters Orientations Toward Subsidiaries in a Multinational Enterprise

Aspects of the Enterprise	Orientation			
	Ethnocentric	*Polycentric*	*Regiocentric*	*Geocentric*
Complexity of organization	Complex in home country, simple in subsidiaries	Varied and independent	Highly interdependent on a regional basis	Increasingly complex and highly interdependent on a world-wide basis
Authority and decision making	High in headquarters	Relatively low in headquarters	High regional headquarters and/or high collaboration among subsidiaries	Collaboration of headquarters and subsidiaries around the world
Evaluation and control	Home standards applied for persons and performance	Determined locally	Determined regionally	Standards which are universal and local
Rewards and punishments; incentives	High in headquarters; low in subsidiaries	Wide variation; can be high or low rewards for subsidiary performance	Rewards for contribution to regional objectives	Rewards to international and local executives for reaching local and world wide objectives

Aspects of the Enterprise	Orientation			
	Ethnocentric	*Polycentric*	*Regiocentric*	*Geocentric*
Communication; information flow	High volume of orders, commands, advice to subsidiaries	Little to and from headquarters; little among subsidiaries	Little to and from corporate headquarters, but may be high to and from regional headquarters and among countries	Both ways and among subsidiaries around the world
Geographical identification	Nationality of owner	Nationality of host country	Regional company	Truly worldwide company, but identifying with national interests
Perpetuation (recruiting, staffing, development)	People of home country developed for key positions everywhere in the world	People of local nationality developed for key positions in their own country	Regional people developed for key positions anywhere in the region	Best people everywhere in the world developed for key positions everywhere in the world

SOURCE: D. A. Heenan and H. V. Perlmutter, *Multinational Organization Development* (Reading, MA: Addison-Wesley, 1979), pp. 18–19.

limited to specific regions of the world. This approach allows the MNC to tailor its policies and practices to specific areas yet limit the number of unique policies and procedures.

Because firms vary from one another as they go through the stages of international development, we find a wide variety of matches between human resource approach and organizational structure. Almost half the firms surveyed by Dowling reported that the operations of the human resource function were unrelated to the nature of the firms' international operations.[41] In some cases an MNC may use a combination of approaches. For example, it may operate its European interests in a regiocentric manner and its Southeast Asian interests in an ethnocentric way until there is greater comfort in operating in that region of the world. Dowling's survey results are shown in Exhibit 2–3.

THE ROLE OF HRM
IN STRATEGIC PLANNING

Recent literature has focused increasingly on links between HRM and strategic issues.[42] Indeed, Lorange asserts that HRM is a critical dimension of strategic management that should be managed in a proactive manner. "Without the growth of human resources as a strategic resource within a corporation," he argues, "it will be difficult to secure the long-term strategic future of the corporation, even though financial resources might be adequate."[43] This argument holds true for the MNC.

Just as international HRM is a field in its infancy, so too is the role of international HRM in strategic planning. The limited empirical research focuses on human resource managers' involvement in formulating and implementing intended strategy. Some writers place the international HRM role in the context of control. For example, Doz and Prahalad[44] advocate a strong HRM process to ensure the planned development of a large enough pool of young executives to allow staffing flexibility, to provide checks and balances in the complex matrix structure, and to allow an explicit linkage of strategic control configurations with executive appointments.

In a recent survey by the authors,[45] the major challenges for the international HRM function in strategic planning included:

▶ Identifying top management potential early.
▶ Identifying critical success factors for the future international manager.

EXHIBIT 2-3   Structure of Human Resources Function

Question

Is the Human Resources function structured in a similar way to the company's international operations?

Answer	n	%
Yes	19	55.9
No, the structure of the HR function is different.	14	44.1

If your answer is No, please describe the structure of your HR function:

n	Response
4	Consulting arrangements from central company; international organization is very small, so HR support provided from U.S.; all offshore HR people report to U.S. headquarters; centralized
2	Corporate HR philosophy developed at world HQ and implemented regionally, considering each region's needs
2	International personnel organization with responsibilities for all personnel activities outside the U.S.
1	Small corporate group of HR professionals; professionals in each strategic business unit and at locations
1	Separate corporate, group, and division int. HR functions; all work closely together on a dotted-line basis, although each area has core responsibilities unique to that level
1	Decentralized HR function; HR unit in each operating unit and in world area regional HQ
1	Depending on size of operation, there may be a local HR function; all expatriates and TCNs on head office payroll handled by group HR
1	HR support to international division is provided through corporate functions
1	Separate personnel departments in each company plus a central/functional personnel group

---

SOURCE: P. J. Dowling, "Hot Issues Overseas," *Personnel Administrator*, Vol. 34, No. 1 (1989), p. 70.

▶ Providing developmental opportunities.

▶ Tracking and maintaining commitments to individuals in international career paths.

▶ Tying strategic business planning to human resource planning and vice versa.

▸ Dealing with the organizational dynamics and multiple (decentralized) business units while attempting to achieve global and regional (for example, Europe) focused strategies.

▸ Providing meaningful assignments at the right time to ensure adequate international and domestic human resources.

Bhatt et al.[46] examined the role of human resource staff and executives in the strategic planning of multinational firms. The study assessed whether and how the human resource department and staff were involved in planning at the corporate and strategic business unit (SBU) levels. The study concluded that human resources involvement at the corporate level tended to be informal, limited in scope, and heavily dependent upon the competence and personal characteristics of the senior human resource executive. The human resource executive thus played a major role separate from the department or functional area. Staffing was the main area in which the human resource executive was involved in strategy formulation; other traditional human resource areas (for example, compensation and evaluation of manager performance) were viewed as general top management concerns and not primarily human resources related. At the SBU level, the human resources department staff was much more involved in strategic planning; its role was more established and the emphasis was on how the human resources staff could help implement a strategy.

SUMMARY

We have, through this discussion, been able to demonstrate that there is an interconnection between international HRM and the stages of internationalization and that structural and strategic imperatives change according to management philosophy and the international business focus of the MNC. International HR managers have a crucial role in effective strategic management. In order to perform this role, they should understand the variations in their firm's development toward a global (even transnational) status. Each growth stage offers new organizational challenges that international HR planning can influence significantly. Anticipating changes in hiring practices, taking a long-term perspective to developing international managers, collecting data, participating in career-path planning, and recognizing potential parent-subsidiary conflict all have implications for both HR planning and policies. The challenges are to be proactive and to create an integrated approach to international HRM that encourages flexibility and local responsiveness.

QUESTIONS

1. What are the stages an international business goes through before its final development into a transnational company?
2. Once a MNC reaches the global developmental stage, what tensions develop between headquarters and subsidiaries?
3. How does a "matrix" structure support the fifth stage of a MNC's global development?
4. What are the different practices associated with ethnocentric, polycentric, regiocentric, and geocentric human resource management approaches?
5. What role can international HRM play in strategic corporate planning?

FURTHER READING

1. C. A. Bartlett, "Building and Managing the Transnational: The New Organizational Challenge," in *Competition in Global Industries*, ed. M. E. Porter. Boston: Harvard Business School Press, 1986, pp. 367–404.
2. Y. Doz, *Strategic Management in Multinational Companies*. London: Oxford Press, Pergamon, 1986. J. R. Galbraith, and R. K. Kazanjian, *Strategy Implementation: Structure, Systems and Process*. St. Paul, Minn.: West Publishing Co., 1986.
3. S. R. Gates and W. G. Egelhoff, "Centralization in Headquarters-Subsidiary Relationships," *Journal of International Business Studies*, Summer 1986, pp. 71–92.
4. F. Ghadar and N. J. Adler, "Management Culture and the Accelerated Product Life Cycle," *Human Resource Planning*, Vol. 12, No. 1 (1989) pp. 37–42.
5. H. V. Perlmutter and D. A. Hedman, "Cooperate to Compete Globally," *Harvard Business Review*, March–April 1986, pp. 136–152.
6. C. K. Prahalad and R. A. Bettis, "The Dominant Logic: A New Linkage Between Diversity and Performance," *Strategic Management Journal*, Vol. 7 (1986) pp. 485–501.
7. M. Schrage, "A Japanese Giant Rethinks Globalization: An Interview with

Yoshihisa Tabushi," *Harvard Business Review*, July–August 1989, pp. 70–76.
8. T. T. Tyebjee, "A Typology of Joint Ventures: Japanese Strategies in the United States," *California Management Review*, Fall 1988, pp. 75–91.

NOTES

1. N. M. Tichy, C. J. Fombrun, and M. A. Devanna, "Strategic Human Resource Management," *Sloan Management Review*, Winter 1982, p. 48.
2. L. Baird and I. Meshoulam, "Managing Two Fits of Strategic Human Resource Management," *Academy of Management Review*, Vol. 13, No. 1 (1988) pp. 116–128.
3. A. V. Phatak, *International Dimensions of Management*, 2nd ed. (Boston, Mass.: PWS-KENT Publishing Co., 1989).
4. Baird and Meshoulam, "Managing Two Fits."
5. Phatak, *International Dimensions.*
6. L. S. Welch and R. Luostarinen, "Internationalization: Evolution of a Concept," *Journal of General Management*, Vol. 14, No. 2 (1988) pp. 34–55.
7. Phatak, *International Dimensions.*
8. "Canadian Licensing Venture Helps Firm Improve Penetration," *Overseas Trading*, Vol. 27, No. 16 (1975) p. 398.
9. Phatak, *International Dimensions.*
10. J. Stopford and L. Wells, *Managing the Multinational* (London: Longmans, 1972).
11. Some firms become involved in exporting through a fortuitous order, and subsequent international activity is relatively unplanned.
12. Stopford and Wells, *Managing the Multinational.*
13. See V. Pucik, "Strategic Human Resource Management in a Multinational Firm," in *Strategic Management of Multinational Corporations: The Essentials*, ed. H. V. Wortzel and L. H. Wortzel (New York: John Wiley, 1985) p. 425.
14. L. Leksell, *Headquarter-Subsidiary Relationships in Multinational Corporations*, Stockholm, 1981.
15. G. Hedlund, "Organization In-between: The Evolution of the Mother-Daughter Structure of Managing Foreign Subsidiaries in Swedish MNCs," *Journal of International Business Studies*, Fall 1984, pp. 109–123.

NOTES

16. S. Ronen, *Comparative and Multinational Management* (New York: John Wiley, 1986).
17. S. F. Slater, N. K. Napier, and M. S. Taylor, "Human Resource Competence as a Source of Competitive Advantage in Multinational Companies: Issues Affecting the Transfer of Distinctive Competence" (Working Paper, Boise State University, 1989).
18. A. R. Negandhi, *International Management* (Newton, Mass.: Allyn and Bacon, 1987).
19. Stopford and Wells, *Managing the Multinational*.
20. See Pucik, "Strategic Human Resource Management," p. 425.
21. Ibid.
22. J. R. Galbraith and R. K. Kazanjian, "Organizing to Implement Strategies of Diversity and Globalization: The Role of Matrix Designs," *Human Resource Management*, Vol. 25, No. 1 (1986) pp. 37–54.
23. Galbraith and Kazanjian, "Organizing to Implement Strategies," p. 50. See also T. T. Naylor, "The International Strategy Mix," *Columbia Journal of World Business*, Vol. 20, No. 2 (1985); and R. A. Pitts and J. D. Daniels, "Aftermath of the Matrix Mania," *Columbia Journal of World Business*, Vol. 19, No. 2 (1984) for a discussion of the matrix form.
24. Galbraith and Kazanjian, "Organizing to Implement Strategies," p. 50.
25. This discussion of centralization and decentralization and control is based on Slater, Napier, and Taylor, "Human Resource Competence."
26. Pucik, "Strategic Human Resource Management."
27. Ibid.
28. Ronen, *Comparative and Multinational Management*.
29. P. J. Dowling, "International HRM," *Human Resource Management: Evolving Roles and Responsibilities*, Vol. 1, ed. L. Dyer. ASPA/BNA Handbook of Human Resource Management series. Washington, D.C.: BNA, 1988.
30. C. A. Bartlett and S. Ghoshal, "Organizing for Worldwide Effectiveness: The Transnational Solution," *California Management Review*, Vol. 31, No. 1 (1988) pp. 54–74.
31. P. Drucker, "The Changing Multinational," *Wall Street Journal*, January 15, 1986, p. 26.
32. Pucik, "Strategic Human Resource Management."
33. P. Lorange, "Human Resource Management in Multinational Cooperative Ventures," *Human Resource Management*, Vol. 25, No. 1 (1986) pp. 133–148.

34. K. Krombeen, "Managing a Global Electronics Company in Tomorrow's World" (Speech delivered at University of Chicago, April 16, 1984).

35. Lorange, "HRM in Multinational Cooperative Ventures."

36. O. Shenkar and Y. Zeira, "International Joint Ventures: Implications for Organization Development," *Personnel Review*, Vol. 16, No. 1 (1987) pp. 30–37.

37. C. A. Bartlett, "How Multinational Organizations Evolve," *Journal of Business Strategy*, Vol. 3, No. 1 (1982). See also T. Hout, M. E. Porter, and E. Rudden, "How Global Companies Win Out," *Harvard Business Review*, Vol. 60, No. 5 (1982).

38. This section is based on D. A. Ondrack, "International Human-Resources Management in European and North-American Firms," *International Studies of Management and Organization*, Vol. 15, No. 1 (1985) pp. 6–32; and Phatak, *International Dimensions*.

39. P. Evans, "The Context of Strategic Human Resource Management Policy in Complex Firms," *Management Forum*, Vol. 6 (1986) pp. 105–117.

40. Ibid.

41. P. J. Dowling, "Hot Issues Overseas," *Personnel Administrator*, Vol. 34, No. 1 (1989) pp. 66–72.

42. For example, L. Dyer, "Bringing Human Resources into the Strategy Formulation Process," in *Perspectives on Personnel/Human Resource Management* (3rd ed.), ed. H. G. Heneman and D. P. Schwab (Homewood, Ill.: Irwin, 1986).

43. Lorange, "HRM in Multinational Cooperative Ventures."

44. Y. Doz and C. K. Prahalad, "Controlled Variety: A Challenge for Human Resource Management in the MNC," *Human Resource Management*, Vol. 25, No. 1 (1986) pp. 55–71.

45. R. S. Schuler and P. J. Dowling, "Survey of ASPA/I Members" (Unpublished manuscript, Stern School of Business, New York University, 1988).

46. B. Bhatt et al., "The Relationship Between the Global Strategic Planning Process and the Human Resource Management Function" in *Readings in Human Resource Management* (3rd ed.), ed. R. S. Schuler, S. A. Youngblood, and V. L. Huber (St. Paul, Minn.: West Publishing Co., 1988) pp. 427–435; and G. Oddou and M. Mendenhall, "Succession-Planning for Global Managers: How Well Are We Preparing Our Future Decision-Makers?" under review at *Business Horizons*.

CHAPTER 3

▼

Recruitment and Selection of International Employees

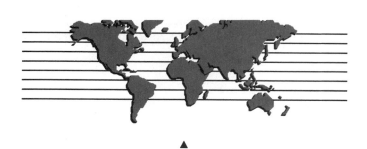

▲

KEY ISSUES IN INTERNATIONAL RECRUITMENT AND SELECTION

The focus of this chapter is on the staffing function and its activities of recruitment and selection in an international context. We define recruitment as searching for and obtaining potential job candidates in sufficient numbers and quality so that the organization can select the most appropriate people to fill its job needs. Selection is the process of gathering information for the purposes of evaluating and deciding who should be employed in particular jobs.[1] The effective utilization of human resources is a goal of most organizations, domestic or international, but there are a number of staffing issues that multinationals must face — executive nationality staffing policies, predictors of expatriate success, expatriate failure, repatriation, equal employment opportunity (EEO), and recruitment and selection of HCNs and TCNs, for example — that are not present in a domestic environment. The aim of this chapter is to critically review the literature on these key issues to identify current and future trends in the recruitment, selection, and transfer of international employees.

EXECUTIVE NATIONALITY STAFFING POLICIES

With regard to executive nationality staffing policies, a multinational company can choose from four options: (1) ethnocentric, (2) polycentric, (3) geocentric, and (4) regiocentric.[2] These policies were discussed in Chapter 2. We shall consider them in detail here because each option has important implications for the recruitment and selection practices of MNCs.

The Ethnocentric Approach

An ethnocentric approach to staffing results in all key positions in a multinational company being filled by parent-country nationals (PCNs). This practice is common in the early stage of internationalization, when a company is establishing a new business, process, or product in another country and prior experience is essential. Other reasons for pursuing an ethnocentric staffing policy are a perceived lack of qualified host-country nationals (HCNs) and the need to maintain good communication links with corporate headquarters. For these reasons, an ethnocentric approach could be perfectly valid for a very experienced MNC that is normally geocentric. For example, a less-developed country (LDC) may specifically request that, as part of a development program, a technology transfer approach using more PCNs be incorporated.

An ethnocentric policy, however, has a number of disadvantages. Zeira[3] has identified several major problems. First, an ethnocentric staffing policy limits the promotion opportunities of HCNs, which may lead to reduced productivity and increased turnover among that group. Second, the adaptation of expatriate managers to host countries often takes a long time, during which PCNs often make mistakes and make poor decisions. Third, when PCN and HCN compensation packages are compared, the often-considerable income gap in favor of PCNs is viewed by HCNs as unjustified. Finally, for many expatriates a key overseas position means new status, authority, and an increase in standard of living. Zeira states that these changes "tend to dull expatriates' sensitivity to the needs and expectations of their host country subordinates — and [are] not conducive to objective self-evaluation."

The Polycentric Approach

A polycentric staffing policy is one in which HCNs are recruited to manage subsidiaries in their own country and PCNs occupy positions at corporate headquarters. There are four main advantages of a polycentric policy. First, employing HCNs eliminates language barriers, avoids the adjustment problems of expatriate managers and their families, and removes the need for expensive training programs. Second, employment of HCNs allows a multinational company to take a lower profile in sensitive political situations. Related to this point, Robinson[4] has noted that a dubious reason for employing local managers is to insulate parent-company personnel from direct involvement in making extralegal payments to local government officials. It is difficult to evaluate the extent to which this factor may influence staffing decisions, but, clearly, in some countries it may well be the case. A third advantage of a polycentric policy is that the employment of HCNs is less expensive, even if a premium is paid to attract high-quality applicants. Fourth, a polycentric policy gives continuity to the management of foreign subsidiaries.

Some of these advantages address some of the shortcomings of an ethnocentric policy. A polycentric policy, however, has its own disadvantages. Perhaps the major difficulty is that of bridging the gap between the local national subsidiary managers and the parent-country managers at corporate headquarters. Language barriers, conflicting national loyalties, and a range of cultural differences (for example, personal value differences and differences in attitudes to business) may isolate the corporate headquarters staff from the various foreign subsidiaries. The result may be that a multinational firm could become a "federation" of independent national units with nominal links to corporate headquarters, a situation that would make a major strategic shift such as a move to production sharing very difficult to achieve.

A second major problem associated with a polycentric staffing policy concerns the career paths of HCN and PCN managers. Host-country managers have limited opportunities to gain experience outside their own country and cannot progress beyond the senior positions in their own subsidiary. Parent-country managers also have limited opportunities to gain overseas experience. As headquarters positions are held only by PCNs, the senior corporate management group responsible for resource allocation decisions between subsidiaries and overall strategic planning may have little overseas work experience from which to draw. In an increasingly competitive international environment, such lack of experience is a liability. It may also reinforce a cynical view among many PCNs that overseas experience is of little value in terms of career advancement.[5]

The Geocentric Approach

In the geocentric approach to international staffing, the best people are sought for key jobs throughout the organization, regardless of nationality. There are two main advantages of a geocentric staffing policy. First, it enables a multinational firm to develop an international executive cadre and, second, it reduces the tendency of national identification of managers with units of the organization.

The first difficulty in implementing a geocentric policy is that most host countries want foreign subsidiaries to employ their citizens. To achieve this goal, they use their immigration laws to require the employment of HCNs if adequate numbers and skills are available. Most western countries (including the United States) require companies to provide extensive documentation if they wish to hire a foreign national instead of a local national. This documentation can be a time-consuming, expensive, and at times futile process. Second, a geocentric policy can be expensive to implement because of increased training and relocation costs and the need to have a compensation structure with standardized international base pay that may be higher than national levels in many countries. Finally, a geocentric staffing policy requires longer lead times and more centralized control of the staffing process, measures that necessarily reduce the independence of subsidiary management, which may be resisted.

The Regiocentric Approach

A fourth approach to international staffing is a regional policy with regard to executive nationality. The best example of this approach is a regiocentric policy, which Heenan and Perlmutter[6] define as functional rationalization on a more-than-one-country basis. The specific mix varies with the nature of a firm's business and product strategy. Robock and Simmonds[7] give three examples of the ways a company's nature or product strategy influences staffing policies. First, if regional or area expertise (for example, in consumer goods and/or limited product lines) is important, the need for PCNs is low relative to the need for experienced HCNs and third-country nationals (TCNs). Second, when product expertise is important and/or industrial markets are being served, PCNs are used more frequently because of the need for quick access to parent-country sources of supply and technical information. Third, service industries such as banking tend to use relatively large numbers of PCNs, particularly when a firm is serving parent-country multinational clients in foreign locations.

In summary, an MNC can pursue one of four approaches to international staffing. Rather than being systematic in selecting one of these approaches, however, an MNC may just proceed on an ad hoc basis. A better descriptor may be corporate inertia. Robinson[8] has succinctly summarized how an ad hoc basis often develops: "The danger is that the firm will opt for a policy of using parent country nationals in foreign management positions by default, that is, simply as an automatic extension of domestic policy, rather than deliberately seeking optimum utilization of management skills." The practice as Robinson describes it is not unknown among U.S. MNCs, but ad hoc staffing today more typically results in the use of HCNs rather than PCNs. A multinational firm that would be described as following an ad hoc staffing approach will clearly have difficulty developing a consistent organizational human resources strategy that fits with the overall business strategy of the enterprise. Consequently, it will often be poorly placed either to anticipate threats or to profit from opportunities.

PREDICTORS OF EXPATRIATE SUCCESS

Writing in the late 1970s, Newman, Bhatt, and Gutteridge[9] characterized the literature on determinants of expatriate effectiveness as essentially repetitive and anecdotal in nature. They recommended "a moratorium on cross sectional research which reports on organizational and expatriate effectiveness in anecdotal form." Their recommendation has been largely ignored; many recent papers[10] continue to uncritically summarize the existing literature without theoretical or methodological concerns.

Three papers have appeared since Newman, Bhatt, and Gutter- idge's review that merit discussion in some detail. The first is an em- pirical study by Tung[11] on selection practices of eighty U.S. multina- tional companies. Based on a review of the literature on expatriate success, Tung grouped the variables that contribute to expatriate success into four general areas: (1) technical competence on the job, (2) per- sonality traits or relational abilities, (3) environmental variables, and (4) family situation. In all, Tung identified eighteen variables, or cri- teria for selection. The respondents (vice presidents of foreign opera- tions) were asked to indicate whether these criteria were "used and very important," "used but not important," or "not used" in their organi- zations. Using categories reported by Hays,[12] Tung classified overseas job assignments as (1) chief executive officer (CEO), (2) functional head, (3) troubleshooter, and (4) operative.

Some criteria such as "maturity and emotional stability" and "tech- nical knowledge of the business" were commonly used and seen as very important for all four job categories. It is clear from the results, how- ever, that for each job category, some criteria were judged to be more important than others. For example, "communicative ability" was less important for technical jobs (troubleshooter) than for a CEO, although "knowledge of host-country language" was not as important for either of these job categories as for functional head and operative. Presum- ably, individuals in these latter job categories have limited access to translators or are more likely to work with HCNs who do not speak En- glish. Despite the obvious differences in demands between domestic and international operations,[13] a notable proportion of respondents used "the same criteria as other comparable jobs at home" for CEOs, functional heads, and operatives.

Tung also asked respondents to indicate the procedures used by each firm to assess the eighteen selection criteria considered in the study. Few companies formally assessed technical competence — a predictable re- sult, as most expatriates are internal recruits, and ample documentation of technical competence is available from performance appraisal data and personnel records. With regard to assessing family situation, 52 percent of companies interviewed both candidate and spouse for man- agement positions, and 40 percent of companies interviewed both can- didate and spouse for technical positions. Only 1 percent of firms con- ducted no interviews with either the candidate or spouse. These figures for interviews with both candidate and spouse may seem high, but they are less impressive when one considers the fact that inability of the spouse to adjust is the most frequently cited reason for expatriate failure.

The most surprising finding was for assessment of relational ability. Although most companies indicated that relational abilities were important, only 5 percent of firms assessed a candidate's relational ability through a formal procedure (for example, judgment by seniors or psychological appraisal). The research literature shows that relational abilities are positively related to expatriate success, so this failure to assess candidates' relational abilities is an obvious deficiency in the expatriate selection procedures of most of the companies in this study. As discussed in Chapter 5, this deficiency probably reflects top management's judgment either that relational abilities are not important or that technical abilities are more important.

A final aspect of Tung's paper that warrants discussion is her selection and training model, shown in Figure 3–1. There are a number of notable features to her model. First, it raises the issue of executive nationality by first requiring information about whether the position could be filled by a HCN. Second, the model follows a noncompensatory selection strategy that Newman, Bhatt, and Gutteridge[14] note is a lower-risk strategy with regard to selecting expatriates. Third, the model takes a contingency approach to selection and training by recognizing that different expatriate jobs involve varying degrees of interaction with HCNs and durations of stay and that foreign assignment locations vary widely in terms of similarity with the expatriate's own culture. Using this model, Tung analyzed the relationship between type of selection and training procedure used and expatriate failure rate for the companies in her sample. She reports a correlation of $-.63$, indicating that the more rigorous the selection and training procedures used, the lower the failure rate.

A second important paper is a recent review of the expatriate acculturation literature by Mendenhall and Oddou.[15] In reviewing problems in expatriate selection, Mendenhall and Oddou state that a major problem area is the ingrained practice of personnel directors, when selecting potential expatriates, to use the "domestic equals overseas performance equation." The effect of this practice is that little else is of importance in the selection process other than technical expertise and a successful domestic track record. They conclude that the field of expatriate selection and training suffers from two interdependent problems. First, there is an inadequate understanding of the relevant variables of expatriate acculturation, which leads to a second problem, the

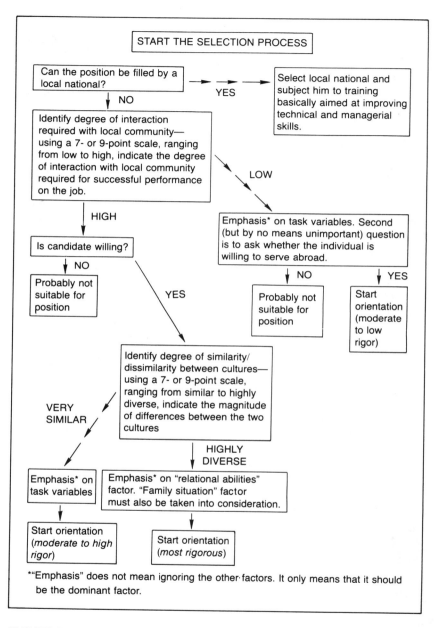

FIGURE 3-1 Flow Chart of the Selection-Decision Process

SOURCE: R. L. Tung, "Selection and Training of Personnel for Overseas Assignments," *Columbia Journal of World Business*, Vol. 16, No. 1 (1981) pp. 68–78.

use of inappropriate selection and training methods. The purpose of their paper was to review the literature to determine the key dimensions involved in the expatriate adjustment process and to examine the implications of these dimensions for the selection and training of expatriates. From their review of the literature, Mendenhall and Oddou conclude that there are four key dimensions in the expatriate adjustment process: (1) self-oriented, (2) others oriented, (3) perceptual, and (4) cultural toughness.

The self-oriented dimension is concerned with activities and attributes that serve to strengthen the expatriate's self-esteem, self-confidence, and mental hygiene. It is composed of three subfactors: (1) reinforcement substitution, (2) stress reduction, and (3) technical competence. Reinforcement substitution involves replacing pleasurable home culture activities and interests with parallel substitutes in the host culture. Thus, an expatriate who is able to adapt his/her interests in food, sports, and music is more likely to be successful in adjusting to the new culture. Stress reduction refers to the need to engage in temporary withdrawal activities (for example, keeping a diary or engaging in favorite activities or hobbies) that allow the expatriate to gradually adjust to the demands of a new cultural and physical environment. The final subfactor is technical competence. Expatriates are expected to accomplish their assigned task; possessing the necessary expertise and confidence in one's ability to achieve this goal (often with little or no assistance) has been shown to be an important part of expatriate adjustment. Mendenhall and Oddou cite a number of studies that found that well-adjusted expatriates report more feelings of expertise in their jobs than do poorly adjusted expatriates.

The others-oriented dimension encompasses activities and attributes that enhance the expatriate's ability to interact effectively with host-country nationals. Two subfactors are involved: relationship development and willingness to communicate. Relationship development refers to the ability to develop long-lasting friendships with host-country nationals. This ability is of assistance to an expatriate in the same way that a mentor is able to assist a neophyte employee. Willingness to communicate does not refer to the level of fluency in a foreign language but rather to the expatriate's confidence and willingness to use the host culture's language. Thus, an expatriate who is not fluent in the host-country language may collect "conversational currency" (local phrases, comments about the weather, sporting terms, and so on) that he/she can use in conversation in order to indicate a desire to understand and relate with host-country nationals.

The perceptual dimension refers to the ability to understand why foreigners behave the way they do. The ability to make correct attributions about the reasons or causes of HCNs' behavior is important because it allows the expatriate to predict future HCN behavior — and reduces the stress of uncertainty in interpersonal relations. According to Mendenhall and Oddou, research has shown that well-adjusted expatriates tend to be nonjudgmental and nonevaluative in interpreting the behavior of host-country nationals, which leads to clearer information exchange and better interpersonal relationships between expatriates and host-country nationals.

The cultural-toughness dimension recognizes the fact that how well the expatriate adjusts to his/her overseas experience appears to be in part related to the country of assignment. The research literature indicates that western expatriates find the cultures of some countries to be more difficult to adapt to than the cultures of other countries. Mendenhall and Oddou cite the work of Torbiorn,[16] who found that western expatriates expressed high levels of dissatisfaction with their overseas assignments in India/Pakistan, Southeast Asia, the Middle East, North Africa, East Africa, and Liberia in the areas of job satisfaction, levels of stress and pressure, health care, housing standards, entertainment, food, and skill of coworkers. It is also important to note that some cultures that emphasize a male-dominated value system may be "extra culturally tough" for western expatriate women to adapt to.

Mendenhall and Oddou derive two major propositions from their study. First, expatriate acculturation is a multidimensional process rather than a unidimensional phenomenon. Thus, selection procedures of multinational firms should be changed from their present one-dimensional focus on technical competence as the primary criterion to a multidimensional focus based on criteria relating to the dimensions identified in their review. Second, comprehensive acculturation training programs incorporating each of the four dimensions outlined above should be designed for expatriates. To carry out these propositions, Mendenhall and Oddou suggest a number of proposals for enhancing the expatriate selection process. Specifically, they recommend that the expatriate selection process should focus on evaluating the applicant's strengths and weaknesses in the dimensions of expatriate acculturation identified in their review:

▸ For the self-oriented dimension, a number of psychological tests are available to measure stress levels and Type A behavior patterns.[17] Technical expertise is already assessed in most organizations.

▸ For the perceptual dimension, psychological tests with established validity could assess the flexibility of an individual's perceptual and evaluative tendencies. They could be used in conjunction with in-depth evaluations from other sources such as a consultant psychologist and the applicant's superiors. Use of testing may also encourage self-reflection regarding motivation for the assignment.

▸ The above approach could also be used to gauge degree of others-orientation.

▸ The toughness of the culture of the country to which a future expatriate will be assigned can be assessed by comparing the host country's political, legal, socioeconomic, and business systems to those in the parent country. If there is considerable disparity (that is, if the host country is "culturally tough"), only applicants with high scores on the battery of evaluation devices should be considered for the assignment. For assignments to countries similar to the parent country (for example, an assignment to Australia from the United States), applicants with more marginal evaluation scores may be considered. This point is very similar to the notion of similarity/dissimilarity between cultures as a selection factor in Tung's model (see Figure 3–1).

In the third study we wish to discuss, Ronen[18] incorporates the dimensions of expatriate success identified by Tung and by Mendenhall and Oddou. In Ronen's model, there are five categories of attributes of success: (1) job factors, (2) relational dimensions (similar to Mendenhall and Oddou's perceptual dimension), (3) motivational state, (4) family situation, and (5) language skills. According to Ronen, however,

> The relative importance of each category is difficult to establish. Returning IAs [international assignees] and managers' evaluations, however, do offer some information in this regard, as reported earlier. Unfortunately, the lack of systematic evaluation of such data renders speculative any statement about the relative importance of these dimensions in contributing to an international assignee's level of effectiveness.

The five categories and their specific aspects are shown in Exhibit 3–1.

EXPATRIATE FAILURE RATES

A prominent issue in the international recruitment and selection literature is that of expatriate failure, which may be defined as the premature return of an expatriate manager. Thus, an expatriate failure

EXHIBIT 3–1   Categories of Attributes of Success

Job Factors
  Technical skills
  Acquaintance with host-country and headquarters operations
  Managerial skills
  Administrative competence

Relational Dimensions
  Tolerance for ambiguity
  Behavioral flexibility
  Nonjudgmentalism
  Cultural empathy and low ethnocentrism
  Interpersonal skills

Motivational State
  Belief in the mission
  Congruence with career path
  Interest in overseas experience
  Interest in the specific host-country culture
  Willingness to acquire new patterns of behavior and attitudes

Family Situation
  Willingness of spouse to live abroad
  Adaptive and supportive spouse
  Stable marriage

Language Skills
  Host-country language
  Nonverbal communication

SOURCE: S. Ronen, "Training the International Assignee," in *Training and Career Development*, ed. I. Goldstein (San Francisco: Jossey-Bass, 1989), p. 438. Used by permission.

represents a false positive selection error.[19] The costs of a false positive selection error are both direct and indirect. In the case of expatriate recalls, the direct costs include salary, training costs, and travel and relocation expenses. Harvey[20] estimates that the average cost per failure to the parent company can be as high as three times the domestic salary plus the cost of relocation, depending on currency exchange rates and location of assignment.

   The importance of indirect or "invisible" costs rises with the level of position in the company. For many expatriate positions, these indirect costs could be considerable. For example, an expatriate head of a foreign subsidiary who subsequently proves to be unsuitable for the job may damage relations with the host-country government and other local organizations and customers, resulting in loss of market share, difficulties with host-government officials, and demands that PCNs be replaced with HCNs. Zeira and Banai[21] argue that multinational corporations should consider these factors, rather than direct expenses such as salary and repatriation costs, as the real cost of failure of international executives.

The international literature also indicates that expatriate failure is a persistent and recurring problem. Mendenhall and Oddou report that the estimated expatriate failure rate from 1965 to the present has fluctuated between 25 percent and 40 percent, and Desatnick and Bennett state that this figure rises to 70 percent in developing countries.[22] In one of the few empirical studies on expatriate failure rates, Tung[23] surveyed a number of U.S., European, and Japanese multinationals. Her results are summarized in Exhibit 3–2.

As Exhibit 3–2 shows, U.S. companies have both higher expatriate failure rates and a higher percentage of companies reporting recall rates of 10 percent or more than European or Japanese multinationals. These national differences, however, should not obscure the fact that all mul-

EXHIBIT 3–2 Expatriate Failure Rates

Recall rate %	*% of companies*
U.S. multinationals	
20–40	7
10–20	69
< 10	24
European multinationals	
11–15	3
6–10	38
< 5	59
Japanese multinationals	
11–19	14
6–10	10
< 5	76

SOURCE: R. L. Tung, "Selection and Training Procedures of U.S., European, and Japanese Multinationals." Copyright © 1982 by the Regents of the University of California. Reprinted from the *California Management Review*, Vol. 25, No. 1, pp. 57–71. By permission of the Regents.

tinationals in Tung's sample reported a significant expatriate failure problem. Although there are no data available that compare domestic and international false positive selection error rates, it would seem reasonable to assume that few companies would report domestic error rates of the relative magnitude shown in Exhibit 3–2.

Some of the differences between domestic and international selection are apparent when reasons for expatriate failure are examined. Tung asked her sample of multinational managers to indicate reasons for expatriate failure in their companies. For U.S. multinationals, the reasons given in descending order of importance were (1) inability of spouse to adjust, (2) manager's inability to adjust, (3) other family problems, (4) manager's personal or emotional maturity, and (5) inability to cope with larger overseas responsibility. For European companies, only one reason was consistently given by respondents to explain expatriate failure: the inability of the manager's spouse to adjust to a new environment. For the Japanese sample the reasons for expatriate failure in descending order of importance were (1) inability to cope with larger overseas responsibility, (2) difficulties with new environment, (3) personal or emotional problems, (4) lack of technical competence, and (5) inability of spouse to adjust. Tung notes that the finding that inability of spouse to adjust was a relatively minor reason in Japanese companies (compared to U.S. and European companies) is not surprising given the role and status to which Japanese society relegates the spouse. As with false positive selection error rates, there are no data available that compare reasons for domestic and international false positive selection errors, but it is a plausible hypothesis that relational and environmental adjustment difficulties would not be as important in explaining the failure of domestic managers as they are for international managers.

As we noted above, expatriate failure is a prominent issue in the international recruitment and selection literature, but there are few empirical studies on expatriate failure. A recent study by Dowling and Welch[24] examining the international HRM policies of four MNCs operating internationally from Australia (two were Australian, one was European, and one was American) found that expatriate failure was not a major concern. All companies in this study reported a small proportion of early recalls, which were attributed as much to lack of technical skills as to the failure of the spouse to adjust. One U.S. personnel director who was interviewed for the study pointed out that attributing expatriate recall to "failure of spouse to adjust" was at times a simplistic explanation. He postulated that, apart from the probability of the expatriate blaming his wife (all the expatriates in this study were male) for his own failure to adjust, some astute spouses may see the expatriate's poor performance and trigger the early recall to limit damage to the expatriate's career. The reported low expatriate failure rates in this study run counter to the pattern in the literature — but the best-known survey on expatriate failure[25] was conducted during the late 1970s. It may well be that since that time companies operating internationally have become more aware of the problems associated with expatriate failure and have learned to avoid them. Clearly, further research on this issue is required.

REPATRIATION

Another issue that is frequently not sufficiently addressed in the international recruitment and selection literature is that of repatriation of expatriates back to their home location at the conclusion of an international assignment. The repatriate employee, and indeed the entire repatriate family, may experience "reverse culture shock" upon return to the home country, as the environment is no longer familiar to them and they may feel somewhat alienated from their surroundings.[26] The repatriate employee may experience professional as well as personal reentry difficulties. Research has indicated several factors that may cause difficulties for repatriates:[27]

▸ The experience of being "out of sight, out of mind" of the parent company may limit chances for promotion upon reentry. Often the company has done little or no planning for the manager's repatriation and career progression.

▸ Managers may experience negative career progression upon reentry if they return to a less challenging job with less responsibility and status than their previous international assignment entailed. Research by Tung[28] has indicated that negative career moves after international experience are evident in many U.S. MNCs. This phenemenon is in contrast to the majority of European, Japanese, and Australian MNCs, which place more importance on international experience. (The U.S. companies tend to focus more readily on the domestic market, while the companies operating from countries with smaller domestic markets must rely more heavily on international markets for revenue.)

▸ Technological advances in the company may render the repatriate's functional skills and knowledge obsolete.

▸ Changes in the formal and informal operations and information channels in the organization may cause adjustment difficulties for the repatriate, particularly if there was insufficient contact with the expatriate during the overseas assignment. Lack of contact creates a sense of isolation and "exile" for the expatriate.

▸ As Adler[29] has reported, 20 percent of the employees who complete overseas assignments want to leave their company on their return. Failure to address repatriation problems may lead to disillusionment and turnover, particularly when many other companies are willing to pay a premium for an expatriate's experience and expertise.[30] The costs to MNCs of expatriate turnover are considerable, in terms of both the loss of valuable employees with international experience to competitors and the investment required to recruit suitable replacements. An additional problem is that fellow employees who witness the difficulties that many repatriates face may become more reluctant to accept international assignments.

For the expatriate spouse and family, reentry may involve difficulties and disillusionment. People may feel alienated in their own country, particularly if they have been out of contact with family, friends, and local events. Their international experience may have distanced them socially and psychologically from their home environment. Expatriates and their families may have enjoyed participation in a social and economic elite during their international assignment, and the return home may bring with it some measure of social disappointment — as well as a compensation package that does not include expatriate premiums (see Tremayne[31]). In addition, repatriates may have developed a broader cultural perspective, as they can compare home-country conditions with other ways of life and environments. Many repatriates report that people show little interest in hearing about their expatriate experiences, which can make conversation uncomfortable.[32]

As several researchers have noted, very few companies have established programs to assist employees and their families with repatriation difficulties.[33] Programs that assist in social and business repatriation should be implemented as part of the overall process of career development and international human resource management. Tung[34] provides some recommendations for successful repatriation:

▸ A mentor program should be established to monitor the expatriate's career progression throughout international and parent-country experience.

▸ If a one-on-one program is not economically viable, the organization should consider the establishment of a HRM unit for career planning, with regular meetings with expatriates and repatriates.

▶ Organizations should maintain contact with expatriates by sending newspapers, company newsletters, and mail, for example.

Harvey[35] proposes repatriation programs to assist in the development of organizational policy and job definition for repatriates and to provide financial and career counseling and family orientation. Such solutions have relatively low costs (particularly when compared to the costs of losing the employee) and are essentially based on improved planning and communication. Until such programs are offered, MNCs lose the knowledge and experience that repatriates can impart to the organization.

EQUAL EMPLOYMENT OPPORTUNITY ISSUES

In the recruitment and selection process, MNCs must address the issue of equal employment opportunity (EEO) for employees in all employment locations. The legal definition and coverage of relevant laws are immediate problems. The United States has one comprehensive statute (Title VII of the Civil Rights Act of 1964) to cover most EEO situations, but many countries (for example, Britain and Australia) have separate legislation to cover racial and sex discrimination (generally reflecting the much later development in other countries of the debate about the position of women in society). Some countries have little or no EEO legislation, particularly in parts of the Middle East, Africa, Asia, and Latin America, where women tend to have a lower social status and are not universally employed.[36] Equal employment opportunity laws are expressions of social values with regard to employment and reflect the values of a society or country. The selection procedures of MNCs often must be defended against illegality and must take into consideration the increasingly conflicting national laws on employment. For example, mandatory retirement/hiring ages are illegal in the U.S. and some other countries but legal in still other countries. Determining which law applies where, and which has precedence, is a problem without a specific solution.

To date, very few women have been sent on expatriate assignments by western MNCs. Adler[37] conducted a survey of international HR practices in over 600 U.S. and Canadian companies and found that of the 13,338 expatriates identified, only 3 percent (402) were female. Female expatriates tended to be employed by companies with over 1,000 employees in the banking, electronics, petroleum, and publishing industries. One explanation that could be offered with regard to these data is that the data simply reflect the preferences of males and females, and the majority of females do not wish to be sent on an expatriate assignment. Such an explanation assumes that both males and females are offered the opportunity of expatriate assignments, which Adler reports is not the case. Another explanation (also offered for minority groups) is that the data reflect the limited number of females with sufficient experience to be sent abroad.

Another explanation is that many MNCs are concerned with the various social norms with regard to women that prevail in many countries. For example, some Middle Eastern countries would not issue a work visa to a female expatriate even if the MNC selected her. Adler argues that such examples are the exception rather than the rule, and in many countries social norms regarding the role of women do not apply to female expatriates because they are seen by locals as foreigners. Expatriate women may be exempt in many situations, but the disadvantages of being a minority cannot be entirely dismissed. For example, some of the traditional methods of entertainment in Asian business culture involve the sexual exploitation of women and clearly exclude female colleagues.

An important issue related to the selection of either male or female expatriates is that of dual-career problems. Dual-career families have been estimated to include 47 million people in the United States,[38] and work-family strains have become an increasing concern for both organizations and individuals. The issues and problems related to balancing the demands of work and family life are escalated when international assignments are involved.[39] Moving one employee overseas for a prolonged assignment may interrupt the spouse's career and children's education and involve much emotional and social upheaval. A further complexity with regard to a spouse's career is that even if a MNC arranges a job for a spouse, there is no guarantee that a work visa will be issued by the host government for this person. Adler[40] has reported that dual-career problems are slightly more of an issue for females offered overseas assignments than for males, but clearly this is an issue for males also.

Equal opportunity for female HCNs is a complex issue for MNCs. Many MNCs already experience difficulties in the recruitment and selection of HCNs, particularly in less-developed countries where relatively low educational and economic levels limit the sources of potential talent.[41] The relative status of women in some countries may further restrict employment practices, particularly EEO objectives. In western countries, the tendency is toward opening all occupations to both sexes, mainly through the introduction of sex discrimination legislation.[42] In general, however, the less developed the country, the less equal are the sexes with regard to job opportunities and education. There are many countries in which the customs, attitudes, or religion are hostile to the presence of women in the professions or business and in society in general. Ball and McCulloch[43] provide details of sexist legislation in several countries, including Pakistan, Saudi Arabia, and India. Even in countries where legislation states that there should be equality of the sexes, the reality may not comply with this. As Jelinek and Adler[44] have stated, the cultures of countries, particularly many Asian countries, "perpetuate the scarcity of indigenous female managers."

Several researchers have focused on the opportunities for foreign MNCs operating in Japan to employ female HCNs.[45] Many MNCs have difficulty attracting well-qualified Japanese women due to cultural reasons and traditional employment arrangements provided by Japanese corporations, so MNCs should consider employing Japanese women for managerial positions. According to Kaminski and Paiz, over one-third of Japanese women hold university or college degrees, but they are not actively recruited by Japanese companies because of cultural preferences for hiring males. Compared to the United States, Japanese women have a relatively low workforce participation rate, and they are mainly employed in traditional occupations (as secretaries, hostesses, or teachers, for example). Although they tend to have good educational qualifications, professional women in Japanese companies play a temporary or support role and do not advance as men do. In the Japanese economy, a full employment policy and lifetime employment are available only to men.[46] The corporate expectation is that women will leave the workforce by the age of 25 to raise a family and may return ten or twenty years later in a part-time position. Japanese national statistics, however, indicate that this employment pattern for females is changing as more women obtain qualifications and remain in the workforce for longer periods.

The limited opportunities and wage disparity for women employed in Japanese companies should assist foreign MNCs in recruiting female employees. Another important factor influencing the need for MNCs to consider hiring females is that the (predominantly male) elite in Japan and many other countries would prefer employment in the civil service or a leading company rather than work for a foreign MNC. Although the idea of women holding managerial level positions is relatively new in Japan, Kaminski and Paiz predict an evolutionary increase in the participation rate of women in the Japanese workforce, particularly as professionals in foreign MNCs. Such a pattern is likely to develop in many other countries as well. As Adler[47] concludes, "There is no doubt that the most successful North American companies will draw on both men and women to manage their international operations. The only question is how quickly and how effectively companies will manage the introduction of women into the worldwide managerial work force."

RECRUITMENT AND SELECTION OF HCNs AND TCNs

As Heenan and Perlmutter,[48] Berenbeim,[49] and other writers have observed, over time a MNC will tend to move from a dominantly ethnocentric staffing policy to a polycentric and/or regiocentric policy. One effect of both polycentric and regiocentric policies is to markedly reduce the number of PCNs sent on overseas assignments. There are a number of reasons why a MNC would want to reduce the population of PCN employees on overseas assignments. One obvious factor is the cost of maintaining expatriates and their families abroad. Combined with base salary levels and various benefits is the cost of taxation in the foreign location, which can become prohibitive for a long assignment. (See Chapter 5 for a detailed summary of the various allowances that are paid to expatriates.) Harvey[50] has estimated that the direct costs of expatriates are three times the domestic salary plus relocation expenses; in Japan, where both housing costs and taxation rates are very high, this figure may be higher. By replacing PCNs with HCNs or TCNs, MNCs can achieve substantial savings.

A second reason why MNCs are often quite willing to replace PCNs is that managerial and technical competence has increased in many countries, and there are now large numbers of qualified and experienced local employees to take the place of expatriate employees. Thus, many MNCs are finding that one of the important reasons for initially using PCNs (lack of suitably qualified local employees) no longer applies. Hiring HCNs also avoids many of the well-documented problems of pursuing an ethnocentric staffing policy of over-reliance on PCNs (see Zeira[51]). As Kobrin[52] has succinctly noted, "all things being equal, a local national who speaks the language, understands the culture and the political system, and is often a member of the local elite should be more effective than an expatriate alien."

A third factor that has often heavily influenced MNC staffing policy has been the pressure from many governments to limit the number of PCNs and increase the number of HCNs. This pressure may be explicit (immigration visa quotas for PCNs) or implicit (informal comments by government officials during negotiations to obtain various licenses or approvals for projects). Thus, many newly developing countries in Asia and Africa require MNCs to commit themselves to extensive training of HCNs before PCN employees are given work visas. In some countries this process is complicated by local political issues. For example, Malaysia has an affirmative action program for the local Malay people, the largest ethnic group who now dominate the government but tend to be underrepresented in the professions and business world relative to the Chinese. Multinational companies that are unable or unwilling to come to terms with the Bumiputra policy (named for the indigenous people in the local Bahasa Malay language) are unlikely to be successful in Malaysia.

This use of immigration regulations is not limited to newly developing countries. Most industrialized countries (including the United States) have immigration rules that require companies to demonstrate why they need to hire a foreign national rather than a local national. Successful MNCs incorporate such requirements into their planning process when they are considering new investments or developments. For example, in the mid 1980s Australia offered a once-only opportunity for foreign banks to enter the local market, and Citibank was one of the successful applicants for a banking license. Banks, along with oil and construction companies, remain heavy users of PCN employees because all three industries require very specific (sometimes firm-specific) skills frequently not found in foreign locations. Over a year before the licenses were to be awarded. Citibank sent one of its senior HR managers on a year-long assignment to Sydney to assess the staffing implications of an application to the Australian government for a banking license. Once an assessment was made as to how many PCN visas would be required, a detailed summary was prepared for the immigration department showing the history of Citibank's investment in training Australian nationals (Citibank already held a limited banking license that allowed it to operate a merchant banking operation and finance company), with career examples of Australian nationals who were now employed by Citibank in Australia, other foreign locations, and in the United States. This proved to be a successful strategy: Citibank received one of the sixteen licenses on offer and all of the visas it requested and is now one of the leading foreign banks in Australia.

The same general criteria for selecting PCNs apply to selecting HCNs, although more training is usually needed, as HCNs often lack detailed knowledge of the organization and its products or services. Desatnick and Bennett[53] emphasize the importance of careful preparation, plus the investment of time and effort, in the recruitment and selection of HCNs. This process involves a realistic assessment of the skills available in the local labor market and the ability to tailor the recruitment and selection process to fit local conditions. For example, college recruiting is an integral part of U.S. recruitment practice, but this is much less the case in other western countries, where business tends to have fewer direct links with educational institutions.

Multinational companies need to utilize the recruitment sources used by local companies, and these sources may not be readily apparent without assistance from a local national personnel manager. To attract the best of the local university graduates, MNCs generally need to offer higher compensation packages than local companies. (See Chapter 5 for a more detailed discussion of compensation issues.) Local national blue-collar workers and clerical employees are usually not as difficult to recruit as managers, but careful planning and identification of staffing needs at every level are still important aspects of the recruitment and selection process. Multinationals must inform themselves of relevant employment laws and requirements when employing HCNs. For example, many countries levy a payroll tax (usually 1 to 2.5 percent of the total payroll) that all companies must pay. This tax is often rebated if the company trains local employees. Negotiations of such rebates usually require the services of a senior HCN manager to represent the MNC or assist PCN managers when meeting with local government officials.

Multinational companies have found advantages in recruiting TCNs because they tend to cost less (few countries have higher managerial wage structures than the United States) and they often come from a country similar to the MNC's home country. Recently, international compensation professionals have noted that as globalization expands as a trend, management salaries across national boundaries are starting to move in line with U.S. rates. Recently, the British Personnel Association pointed out the significant increase in U.K. management salaries. One of the reasons was reported to be that the British head of a U.S. subsidiary will no longer accept a U.S. subordinate with a higher salary. Even with salary equity, however, TCNs can be cheaper because of the impact of U.S. income taxes. The United States is one of the few countries that taxes its nationals employed overseas. Thus, U.S., Australian, and British expatriates working side by side in Taiwan might have similar salaries and take-home pays, but the U.S. expatriate costs more because the employer doesn't have to worry about Australian or British income tax. Not only is the American employee's salary taxable in Taiwan, but his/her salary and allowances such as housing and relocation expenses (paid on the employee's behalf) are taxable in the United States as well. Thus, the cost of the American employee includes the raw salary plus tax equalization or tax protection, which, in some high-tax countries, can cost the employer more than the employee's salary.[54]

American MNCs also find it advantageous to hire TCNs who have already been working for the organization and thus are familiar with its management policies and practices. In addition, TCNs are unlikely to experience conflict between loyalty to the organization and loyalty to the host country. (Ball and McCulloch[55] provide examples of HCNs giving preference to local suppliers when imported goods were less expensive and of superior quality.)

Not surprisingly, one difficulty of hiring TCNs is that host countries that place importance on employment of their own citizens may regard the employment of large numbers of TCNs to be as unacceptable as a large number of PCNs. Third-country nationals tend to be most numerous where a MNC has established a regional headquarters (for example, a Pacific Basin regional headquarters in Melbourne or Singapore), as employees from countries in the region are assigned to the regional headquarters to gain wider experience or to fill specific positions.

In a recent controversial article, Kobrin[56] argues that many U.S. companies have overdone the replacement of U.S. expatriates with HCNs. In addition to the reasons discussed above (lowering costs, responding to local pressures, and so on) Kobrin believes that U.S. MNCs may have substituted HCNs and TCNs for expatriates in response to "the difficulties that Americans have had in adjusting to other cultural environments rather than for the usual reasons of effectiveness and efficiency. . . . Put directly, Americans may not have been able to handle international assignments and many U.S. firms may have 'solved' the problem by virtually getting out of the expatriate business." He argues that, in doing so, U.S. MNCs could become composed primarily of employees who identify with the local subsidiary rather than the worldwide organization. Such conditions raise major strategic management and control issues such as how to encourage managers to identify with firm-wide rather than local objectives, how to maintain strategic control over personnel and the informal organization, and how to internationalize U.S. managers if they are not sent on expatriate assignments.

Kobrin's explanation as to why American managers are not being sent on expatriate assignments has major implications for the recruitment, selection, and training of managers in U.S. MNCs. He notes that "the problem is exacerbated by the scandalously low levels of international awareness and language competence found in graduates of American universities and business schools," which may be another difficulty U.S. MNCs must face when they recruit future managers. This latter point is reinforced by a recent Gallup poll conducted for the National Geographic Society that surveyed 18- to 24-year-olds from nine countries.[57] American respondents in this survey were ranked *last* in terms of general geographic knowledge (a variable that would correlate reasonably well with "international awareness").

American MNCs may have to become more selective in their recruiting by emphasizing international awareness, language skills,[58] and so on and investing more heavily in training to develop an international cadre of managers. They may also have to consider increasing the number of TCNs, whom they recruit at U.S. schools.[59] There is some evidence to indicate that some U.S. MNCs are aware of the issues discussed by Kobrin. In a recent survey of U.S. managers responsible for international HRM, respondents rated issues such as "the necessity to learn to think globally" and "the changing role of the U.S. expatriate in the world" among the most important current issues in international HRM.[60] Even with a sufficient cadre of qualified expatriates, however, U.S. MNCs are increasing their use of TCNs and HCNs mainly for cost and political reasons. As they do, the issues of training and retaining TCNs and HCNs will grow in importance and MNCs will have to give more consideration to career opportunities and career paths for TCNs and HCNs, as described in Chapter 5.

SUMMARY

This chapter has identified a number of issues and trends in the area of international staffing. First, there is a need for more detailed empirical work that builds on the existing literature. For example, the work of Tung[61] suggests that expatriate failure is a general problem for many MNCs and, it would appear, a particular problem for U.S. MNCs. Future research should, first, confirm whether expatriate failure continues to be a major staffing issue and, second, examine the incidence of failure by job category (CEO, functional head, operative, or trouble-shooter) to determine the extent of the problem for each category and whether reasons for failure vary by job category. In addition, the model of expatriate acculturation proposed by Mendenhall and Oddou[62] could be tested by examining case histories of successful and unsuccessful expatriates or through a more formal empirical validation strategy.

Second, there is a need for studies that examine new ways to select expatriates. Since most expatriates are selected from within the company, the use of an internal staffing technique such as an assessment center should be considered. Mendenhall and Oddou have suggested that this may be a useful technique to use for measuring the personal dimensions (self-oriented, perceptual, and others-oriented) of their model.[63] Other internal staffing techniques such as the use of a selection board composed of managers with recent experience overseas should also be examined.[64]

Third, as noted by Newman, Bhatt, and Gutteridge,[65] researchers should differentiate between organizations that follow a compensatory selection strategy and those that use a noncompensatory strategy. Given the limited research on predictors of successful expatriates, requiring a degree of competency on all relevant selection criteria (a noncompensatory strategy) should be a lower-risk strategy. The model proposed by Tung (see Figure 3–1) is a noncompensatory model, although she does not specifically identify this as a feature of the model.

A fourth area that needs to be addressed by researchers is the influence (or lack of influence) of human resource planning on international staffing. Torbiorn[66] has noted the impact of lack of planning in this area: "The mass of possible selection criteria proposed in the literature is rarely likely to be matched by a wide range of available candidates and the man chosen is often simply the man who happens to be there." Such situations are inevitable at times, but this cannot be a permanent strategy. Mendenhall and Oddou[67] have also noted that too often expatriates are hurriedly selected because of the need to resolve a staffing crisis in an overseas subsidiary. To address this situation, they argue, top management would need to provide institutional and political support in three areas: First, the personnel department must have accurate forecasts of staffing needs in foreign subsidiaries; second, the length of time budgeted for the selection and training process must be increased; and third, expatriate selection and training should begin early in a manager's career so that the organization can develop a pool of internationally oriented managers.

QUESTIONS

1. Outline the main characteristics of the ethnocentric, polycentric, regiocentric, and geocentric approaches to international staffing.
2. What are the main advantages and disadvantages of a polycentric approach to international staffing?
3. Why is an ad hoc approach to international staffing invariably a dysfunctional strategy for MNCs?
4. What are the most important criteria MNCs should use when selecting PCNs? What factors may influence these criteria?
5. Many MNCs perceive serious limitations with regard to assigning female managers to overseas locations. What are these perceived limitations, and do you think these perceptions will change over time?

FURTHER READING

1. P. L. Blocklyn, "Developing the International Executive," *Personnel*, March 1989, pp. 44–48.
2. R. Brislin et al., *Intercultural Interactions, A Practical Guide*. Beverly Hills, Calif.: Sage, 1986.
3. P. J. Dowling and T. W. Nagel, "Nationality and Work Attitudes: A Study of Australian and American Business Majors," *Journal of Management*, Vol. 12 (1985) pp. 99–106.
4. W. A. Evans, D. Sculli, and W. S. L. Yau, "Cross-cultural Factors in the Identification of Managerial Potential," *Journal of Management*, Vol. 13, No. 1 (1987) pp. 52–59.
5. P. R. Harris and R. T. Morgan, *Managing Cultural Differences*, 2nd ed. Houston, Tex.: Gulf, 1979.
6. R. M. Hodgetts and F. Luthans, "Japanese HR Management Practices," *Personnel*, April 1988, pp. 42–45.
7. R. B. Ondrack and H. F. Schwind, "A Comparative Study of Personnel Problems in International Companies and Joint Ventures in Japan," *Journal of International Business Studies*, Spring–Summer 1977, pp. 45–55.
8. K. S. Savich and W. Rodgers, "Assignment Overseas: Easing the Transition Before and After," *Personnel*, August 1988, pp. 44–48.

NOTES

1. R. S. Schuler and V. L. Huber, *Personnel and Human Resource Management*, 4th ed. (St. Paul, Minn.: West Publishing Co., 1990).

2. See R. D. Robinson, *International Business Management: A Guide to Decision Making*, 2nd ed. (Hinsdale, Ill.: Dryden, 1978); D. A. Heenan and H. V. Perlmutter, *Multinational Organization Development* (Reading, Mass.: Addison-Wesley, 1979); and S. H. Robock and K. Simmonds, *International Business and Multinational Enterprises*, 4th ed. (Homewood, Ill.: Irwin, 1989).

3. Y. Zeira, "Management Development in Ethnocentric Multinational Corporations," *California Management Review*, Vol. 18, No. 4 (1976) pp. 34–42.

4. Robinson, *International Business Management*.

5. See L. Smith, "The Hazards of Coming Home," *Dun's Review*, October 1975, pp. 71–75.

6. Heenan and Perlmutter, *Multinational Organization Development*.

7. Robock and Simmonds, *International Business and Multinational Enterprises*.

8. Robinson, *International Business Management*, p. 297.

9. J. Newman, B. Bhatt, and T. Gutteridge, "Determinants of Expatriate Effectiveness: A Theoretical and Empirical Vacuum," *Academy of Management Review*, Vol. 4 (1978) pp. 655–661.

10. For example, see J. E. Heller, "Criteria for Selecting an International Manager," *Personnel*, Vol. 57, No. 3 (1980) pp. 47–55; C. Raffael, "How to Pick Expatriates," *Management Today*, April 1982, pp. 59–62; and F. T. Murray and A. H. Murray, "Global Managers for Global Businesses," *Sloan Management Review*, Vol. 27, No. 2 (1986) pp. 75–80.

11. R. L. Tung, "Selection and Training of Personnel for Overseas Assignments," *Columbia Journal of World Business*, Vol. 16, No. 1 (1981) pp. 68–78.

12. R. D. Hays, "Expatriate Selection: Insuring Success and Avoiding Failure," *Journal of International Business Studies*, Vol. 5, No. 1 (1974) pp. 25–37.

13. P. J. Dowling, "International and Domestic Personnel/Human Resource Management: Similarities and Differences," in *Readings in Personnel and Human Resource Management* (3rd ed.), ed. R. S. Schuler, S. A. Youngblood, and V. L. Huber (St. Paul, Minn.: West Publishing Co., 1988).

14. Newman, Bhatt, and Gutteridge, "Determinants of Expatriate Effectiveness."

15. M. Mendenhall and G. Oddou, "The Dimensions of Expatriate Acculturation: A Review," *Academy of Management Review*, Vol. 10 (1985) pp. 39–47. Note that Mendenhall and Oddou's statement assumes that personnel directors are the ones who actually make the "expatriate selection" decision. In many/most cases the "selection" decision is a line management prerogative.

16. I. Torbiorn, *Living Abroad: Personal Adjustment and Personnel Policy in the Overseas Setting* (New York: John Wiley, 1982).

17. For a review of the Type A literature, see V. A. Price, *Type A Behavior Pattern: A Model for Research and Practice* (New York: Academic Press, 1982).

18. S. Ronen, "Training the International Assignee," in *Training and Career Development*, ed. I. Goldstein (San Francisco: Jossey-Bass, 1990), p. 430.

19. For a discussion of selection error, see H. G. Heneman et al., *Personnel/ Human Resource Management*, 4th ed. (Homewood, Ill.: Irwin, 1989). This notion of expatriate failure is by no means clear-cut. According to Pat Morgan, HR professionals have a lot of trouble when discussing "expat failure." They are conscious that they may get tagged with the impact of the additional cost of expat failure as well as the blame associated with it. At a senior HR level, many professionals have great difficulty with the definition or lack of definition of the term "failure"; some say that definitionally, expatriate failure is 100 percent because eventually every expat returns home. What *is* the definition? Is failure totally employee- and dependent-caused, or can it be company caused, in the case, for example, of company reorganization or the death of a senior manager, which may require an expat to return to the home office to fill a vacancy earlier than expected? Many professionals think the subject is overblown.

20. M. G. Harvey, "The Multinational Corporation's Expatriate Problem: An Application of Murphy's Law," *Business Horizons*, Vol. 26, No. 1 (1983) pp. 71–78.

21. Y. Zeira and M. Banai, "Present and Desired Methods of Selecting Expatriate Managers for International Assignments," *Personnel Review*, Vol. 13, No. 3 (1984) pp. 29–35.

22. Mendenhall and Oddou, "The Dimensions of Expatriate Acculturation"; and R. L. Desatnick and M. L. Bennett, *Human Resource Management in the Multinational Company* (New York: Nichols, 1978).

23. R. L. Tung, "Selection and Training Procedures of U.S., European and Japanese Multinationals," *California Management Review*, Vol. 25, No. 1 (1982) pp. 57–71.

24. P. J. Dowling and D. Welch, "International Human Resource Management: An Australian Perspective," *Asia-Pacific Journal of Management*, Vol. 6, No. 1 (1988) pp. 39–65.

25. Tung, "Selection and Training of Personnel for Overseas Assignments."

26. M. G. Harvey, "The Other Side of Foreign Assignments: Dealing with the Repatriation Dilemma," *Columbia Journal of World Business*, Vol. 17, No. 1 (1982) pp. 52–59.

27. See N. J. Adler, *International Dimensions of Organizational Behavior* (Boston: PWS-KENT Publishing Company, 1986); Torbiorn, *Living Abroad;* and R. L. Tung, "Career Issues in International Assignments," *Academy of Management Executive*, Vol. 2, No. 3 (1988) pp. 241–244.

28. Tung, "Career Issues."

29. Adler, *International Dimensions of Organizational Behavior.*

30. See D. W. Kendall, "Repatriation: An Ending and a Beginning," *Business Horizons*, Vol. 24, No. 6 (1981) pp. 21–25.

31. S. Tremayne, "Shell Wives in Limbo," in *The Incorporated Wife*, ed. H. Callan and S. Ardener (Kent, England: Croom Helm, 1984).

32. See Harvey, "The Other Side of Foreign Assignments"; and Tremayne, "Shell Wives in Limbo." See also M. Harvey, "Repatriation of Corporate Executives: An Empirical Study," *Journal of International Business Studies*, Spring 1984; G. Oddou and M. Mendenhall, "The Career Impact of an Overseas Assignment" (Paper presented at the Career Issues in International Management Symposium, Academy of Management, Washington, D.C., August 15, 1989); J. S. Black, "Japanese Repatriation Practices and Results," (Paper presented at the Career Issues in International Management Symposium, Academy of Management, Washington, D.C., August 15, 1989); R. L. Tung, "International Assignments: Strategic Challenges in the 21st Century" (Paper presented at the Career Issues in International Management Symposium, Academy of Management, Washington, D.C., August 15, 1989); R. L. Tung, "Career Issues"; M. Mendenhall and G. Oddou, "The Overseas Assignment: A Practical Look," *Business Horizons*, September–October 1988, pp. 78–84; Korn/Ferry International, "A Study of Repatriation of the American International Executive," New York, 1981; and C. G. Howard, "The Expatriate Manager and the Role of the MNC," *Personnel Journal*, Vol. 48, No. 1 (1973) pp. 25–29.

33. See Adler, *International Dimensions of Organizational Behavior;* Torbiorn, *Living Abroad;* Tung, "Career Issues"; J. S. Black and G. Stephens, "The Influence of the Spouse on American Expatriate Adjustment and Intent to Stay in Pacific Rim Assignments," *Journal of Management*, in press (best paper award of the International Division of the Career Issues in International Management Symposium, Academy of Management, Washington, D.C., August 15, 1989); G. Stephens and J. S. Black, "Impact of Spouse's Career-Orientation on Managers During International Transfers," *Journal of Management Studies*, in press; M. Harvey, "The Executive

Family: An Overlooked Variable in International Assignments," *Columbia Journal of World Business*, Spring 1985, pp. 84–93; M. Gaylord, "Relocation and the Corporate Family," *Social Work*, May 1979, pp. 186–191; and E. J. Walker, "'Til Business Do Us Part?" *Harvard Business Review*, 1976, pp. 94–101.

34. Tung, "Career Issues."

35. M. Harvey, "The Multinational Corporation's Expatriate Problem: An Application of Murphy's Law."

36. See Desatnick and Bennett, *Human Resource Management*.

37. N. J. Adler, "Women in International Management: Where Are They?" *California Management Review*, Vol. 26, No. 4 (1984) pp. 78–89.

38. D. T. Hall and J. Richter, "Balancing Work and Home Life: What Can Organizations Do to Help?" *Academy of Management Executive*, Vol. 2, No. 3 (1988) pp. 213–223.

39. See Harvey, "The Executive Family"; and W. Coyle, *On the Move: Minimizing the Stress and Maximizing the Benefit of Relocation* (Sydney, Australia: Hampden Press, 1988); and Dowling, "International and Domestic Personnel/Human Resource Management."

40. N. J. Adler, "Women Do Not Want International Careers: And Other Myths About International Management," *Organizational Dynamics*, Vol. 13, No. 2 (1984) pp. 66–79. According to Pat Morgan, President, International Chapter of Society of Human Resource Management, there is a lot more discussion today about "trailing spouses." Interestingly, many HR departments are reporting to their peers that when the trailing spouse is a male, the problems are much more difficult because of the male's ego and self-worth issues. These cases are receiving a lot of attention because many enlightened MNCs want to ensure that women do have the opportunity to complete an international assignment and then return to move up the corporate ladder. (Personal communication, August 1989.)

41. Desatnick and Bennett, *Human Resource Management*.

42. See C. E. Landau, "Recent Legislation and Case Law in the EEC on Sex Equality in Employment," *International Labour Review*, Vol. 123, No. 1 (1984) pp. 53–70.

43. D. A. Ball and W. H. McCulloch, *International Business: Introduction and Essentials* (Plano, Tex.: Business Publications, 1988).

44. M. Jelinek and N. J. Adler, "Women: World-Class Managers for Global Competition," *Academy of Management Executive*, Vol. 2, No. 1 (1988) pp. 11–19.

45. M. Kaminski and J. Paiz, "Japanese Women in Management: Where Are They?" *Human Resource Management*, Vol. 23, No. 3 (1984) pp. 277–292; and P. Lansing and K. Ready, "Hiring Women Managers in Japan: An

Alternative for Foreign Employers," *California Management Review*, Vol. 26, No. 4 (1988) pp. 469–481.

46. M. A. Devanna, "Women in Management: Progress and Promise," *Human Resource Management*, Vol. 26, No. 4 (1987) pp. 469–481.

47. N. J. Adler, "Pacific Basin Managers: A Gaijin, Not a Woman," *Human Resource Management*, Vol. 26, No. 2 (1987) pp. 169–191.

48. Heenan & Perlmutter, *Multinational Organization Development*.

49. R. E. Berenbeim, *Managing the International Company: Building a Global Perspective* (New York: The Conference Board, 1983).

50. Harvey, "The Multinational Corporation's Expatriate Problem."

51. Zeira, "Management Development in Ethnocentric Multinational Corporations."

52. S. J. Kobrin, "Expatriate Reduction and Strategic Control in American Multinational Corporations," *Human Resource Management*, Vol. 27, No. 1 (1988) pp. 63–75.

53. Desatnick & Bennett, *Human Resource Management*.

54. Correspondence with Patrick Morgan of Bechtel, August 1989.

55. Ball and McCulloch, *International Business*.

56. Kobrin, "Expatriate Reduction."

57. *Geography: An International Gallup Survey*, a survey conducted for The National Geographic Society (Princeton, N. J.: The Gallup Organization, 1988).

58. A strong case can be made for the proposition that English is now the language of world business, but it is also the case that English speakers who refuse to use any other language are frequently perceived to be ethnocentric in their attitudes and behavior. A number of writers have made the point that bilingualism is *qualitatively* different from monolingualism because it gives a "stereo quality" to perception and interpretation. See G. Hedlund, "The Hypermodern MNC — A Heterarchy?" in *Human Resource Management*, Vol. 25, No. 1 (1988) p. 31, for a discussion of this issue and further references.

59. See B. Luck-Nunke, "Recruiting European Nationals to Return to Their Home Countries," *Personnel Administrator*, July 1984, pp. 41–45.

60. P. J. Dowling, "Hot Issues Overseas," *Personnel Administrator*, Vol. 34, No. 1 (1989) pp. 66–72.

61. Tung, "Selection and Training of Personnel for Overseas Assignments" and "Selection and Training Procedures."

62. Mendenhall and Oddou, "The Dimensions of Expatriate Acculturation."

63. Ibid.

64. See A. L. Hixon, "Why Corporations Make Haphazard Overseas Staffing Decisions," *Personnel Administrator*, Vol. 31, No. 3 (1986) pp. 91–94.

65. Newman, Bhatt, and Gutteridge, "Determinants of Expatriate Effectiveness."

66. Torbiorn, *Living Abroad*, p. 51.

67. Mendenhall and Oddou, "The Dimensions of Expatriate Acculturation."

CHAPTER 4

▼

Performance Appraisal

▲

Once MNCs staff their international operations, they need to appraise the performance of both employees and the operation as a whole. This chapter focuses on performance appraisal in an international context. Although it is similar in some respects to performance appraisal in domestic operations, there are some significant differences. This chapter will highlight these differences.

There are aspects of international business that require a substantial modification of traditional appraisal criteria that have been developed for a domestic business environment. First, HR management must recognize that technical competence is a necessary but not sufficient condition for successful performance in international management positions. Cross-cultural interpersonal skills, sensitivity to foreign norms and values, understanding of differences in labor practices or customer relations, and ease of adaptation to unfamiliar environments are just a few of the managerial characteristics most multinational firms seek and evaluate. Second, in addition to appraising these basic operational and managerial level skills, HR departments must develop an appropriate appraisal system for evaluating managers on attributes associated with successful performance at a strategic level.[1]

Although it may be important to appraise performance in MNCs on the basis of operational, managerial, and strategic criteria, there are major challenges in doing so. For purposes of our discussion, we must distinguish between these criteria in appraising performance. Whereas operational and managerial criteria are more legitimately applied to the evaluation of managerial performance, strategic criteria are more legitimately applied to the evaluation of the subsidiary or foreign affiliate. Despite these distinctions, individual managers may be evaluated according to strategic criteria in addition to operational and managerial criteria because individual managers can have a significant impact on subsidiary performance. As Pucik[2] has noted:

> The successful execution of competitive global strategy requires managers and executives with excellent environment-scanning abilities, familiar with conditions of business and market opportunities not in one, but in a number of countries and regions, and sensitive to special constraints facing multinational corporations, such as the relationship with the host governments. For example, interaction with top government officials and legislators is a function reserved in the home office to the chief executive and his staff. In foreign subsidiaries, the same task may fall on the shoulders of managers a number of layers below the corporate ladder. The proposition that an appraisal on the strategic level ought to be focused on the congruence of current managerial performance with long-term corporate objectives is today widely accepted at least as a theory, while its practical application is often bogged down by the constraint of organizational realities. In what form should long-term goals be expressed to be measurable against performance? What aspects of performance should be considered?

The difficulty in answering these questions makes the appraisal of managerial performance on an international level extremely complex. Because of this difficulty and the fact that they are really more descriptive of the performance of the subsidiary unit, strategic criteria are used here to describe the appraisal process of the unit rather than the individual manager. There is, however, certainly a relationship between the activities of the manager and the subsidiary, so a discussion of the issues related to evaluating the unit is pertinent.

FACTORS ASSOCIATED WITH EXPATRIATE PERFORMANCE AND MANAGERIAL APPRAISAL

The assessment of PCN performance is enhanced by a consideration of the variables that influence a PCN's success or failure in a foreign assignment. The performance of a PCN is influenced by three variables: the environment, the task, and the personality of the individual. The factors associated with the national environment to which a PCN is assigned can be critical to the success of the individual. Variables associated with the particular job to be performed abroad are considered to be task variables. The individual factors are those associated with the characteristics and the situation of the person being considered for the international assignment.[3] After describing these, we can look at some ways in which performance can be appraised.

Environment

The environment has an impact on any job, but it becomes of primary importance in the role of the expatriate. As environments differ greatly, their potential for fostering successful performance also varies. Some environments can yield a relatively easy adaptation by a PCN, while others impose tremendous difficulties. (This is similar to the notion of "cultural toughness" discussed in Chapter 3.) Many factors that can be expected or taken for granted in one's home country may not exist in the host country. It is likely that expatriate managers and their families will have some difficulty adjusting to a new environment, which will impact on the manager's work performance. This difficulty should be taken into account when assessing work performance.

Task

In attempting to predict how well an individual will perform in the expatriate assignment, consideration must be given to the general type of job assignment overseas. That is, the specific task variables should be assessed. Task variables are generally considered to be more under a MNC's control than environmental factors. Because of this relative control, the task variables can be better assessed and more easily changed. Richard Hays[4] categorizes the general types of expatriate assignments into four groups:

▸ The *structure reproducer* carries the assignment of building or reproducing in a foreign subsidiary a structure similar to that which he or she knows from another part of the company. He or she could be building a marketing framework, implementing an accounting and financial reporting system, or establishing a production plant, for example.

▸ The *troubleshooter* is the individual who is sent to a foreign subsidiary to analyze and solve a particular operational problem.

▸ The *operational element* is the individual whose assignment is to perform as an acting element in an already existing operational structure.

▸ The *chief executive officer* has the assignment of overseeing and directing the entire foreign operation.

As various categories of job assignments are examined, it becomes clear that the ability of the individual to perform a particular job is critical to the success of the assignment. It is generally thought that most MNCs are able to obtain a reasonably accurate assessment of an individual's basic capability for the job, in terms of the task involved, from performance evaluations prior to the expatriate assignment. Many individuals and firms rank job ability as the primary ingredient relating to their expected probability of success in the international assignment (the "domestic equals overseas performance equation" mentioned in Chapter 3). Certain types of tasks, however, require significantly more interaction with local culture than others. Thus the task variables and environmental factors can be interrelated. The process of establishing a new marketing system or operating as a chief executive officer, for example, may depend heavily on an individual's ability to interact effectively with the local culture and environment. On the other hand, a technical troubleshooter probably requires considerably less ability to efficiently operate within a foreign environment. Clearly, in job assignments and tasks that require an ability to relate effectively and closely with the local culture, the social and cultural skills of the individual become more critical to the success of the assignment.

Another factor relating to task variables that warrants consideration is the similarity of the job the individual is assigned abroad to the job he or she held domestically. Some types of tasks require an individual to operate within a given structure, while other tasks demand the creation of the structure. Individuals vary greatly in their ability to conceive and implement a system and their tolerance for lack of structure and ambiguity. Some MNCs have experienced failure abroad because they assumed that an individual could be effective in setting up a structure, such as a marketing system, based on evidence of good performance within the existing marketing structure in the domestic corporation.[5]

Personality Factors

Personality factors appear to play a role in explaining an international manager's ability to adapt to a foreign environment. Thus much of the expatriate effectiveness literature is concerned with assessing personality variables. As the environment and the job may be largely predetermined in any particular instance, the choice of the individual is one of the few decisions under the control of the MNC. Personality variables appear to play an important role in helping to increase the probability of successful performance of international managers.[6]

For example, an individual's position along the dogmatism/authoritarianism scale, which can be determined with some accuracy, has a significant influence on his or her performance as an international manager. Dogmatism is a relatively closed conception of beliefs and disbeliefs about reality, and authoritarianism is a preoccupation with power and status considerations and a general hostility toward members' outgroups. Authoritarian personality traits and dogmatism tend to represent one end of the scale; the other end is represented by the corresponding opposites of openness, social sensitivity, and empathy.[7] These variables are relevant to the performance of international managers because open-minded individuals seem to adapt more easily to new environments. Those who score high on authoritarianism/dogmatism often have difficulty accepting and adjusting to a new culture and therefore may be somewhat less effective in accomplishing tasks with the local culture.[8]

In summary, the environment, the job or tasks, and the individual are important factors that interact to narrow the types of expatriate assignment choices with the highest probability of successful peformance. These factors have significant implications for assessing the performance of international managers. The circumstances of a particular assignment will dictate which factors are of primary importance.

CRITERIA USED FOR PERFORMANCE APPRAISAL OF INTERNATIONAL EMPLOYEES

Now that we have an understanding of the variables likely to influence managerial performance, we can discuss the criteria by which performance is to be appraised and evaluated. These criteria are generally a function of the nature of the specific type of expatriate assignment (for example, Hays's structure reproducer, troubleshooter, and so on[9]), the stages of international business development, and the international HRM philosophy or approach of the MNC.

As discussed in Chapter 2, the approach of the MNC to human resource management influences which criteria are used and who sets the standards. With an ethnocentric approach, standards are set and administered by PCNs. With a polycentric approach, standards are largely determined and administered by HCNs at the local level. As the stage of international business development changes, appraisal criteria also change. For example, a change in focus from technology transfer and narrow objectives to a more global approach with longer-term objectives requires a considerable change in emphasis with regard to performance appraisal. The type and relevance of these criteria vary according to the form of control exercised by the parent over the subsidiary. Whether this control is loose or tight, subsidiary performance has implications for the overall financial performance of the MNC. Hence, it is important to understand the issues associated with subsidiary unit appraisal.

First, MNCs commonly use arbitrary transfer pricing and other financial tools for transactions between subsidiaries to minimize foreign-exchange risk exposure and tax expenditures. Thus, the financial results recorded for any particular subsidiary do not always reflect accurately its contribution to the achievements of the corporation as a whole. Therefore, such results cannot and should not be used as a primary input in managerial appraisal.[10]

Second, all financial figures are generally subject to the problem of currency conversion, including sales and cash positions. In a MNC, it may not be known how much is sold in any given time period. Further complications arise because some currencies are not convertible to foreign currencies. For example, a profit of 300 million Indian rupees from that branch operation may be meaningless if you cannot bring the money out of India.[11]

Third, the success of subsidiaries is in many ways a product of the accounting and financial operations of the MNC. An extremely important aspect of both of these disciplines is to give management feedback on results in an accurate, concise way, so that managers know how they are performing and are able to plan properly for the future. In both areas, the international dimension is a rapidly growing area, simply because MNC managers would like to know what is going on. The nature of the international monetary system and local accounting differences, however, preclude an accurate measurement of results. How, then, can the MNC measure results? Many MNCs appear to measure cash flow very precisely. If various subsidiaries, after suitable development periods, are generating healthy cash surpluses, then the MNC is probably performing satisfactorily, regardless of the indications of more traditional accounting ratios. Most MNCs would have little cause for concern if cash deficits were being incurred (as when a major expansion is under way) as long as sufficient credit was available and there were prospects for surpluses in the future. In short, MNC managers work, by necessity, with somewhat cruder evaluative techniques than their domestic counterparts.

The use of transfer pricing and other financial tools is necessary because of the complexity of the international environment. Multinationals cannot allow subsidiaries to become autonomous in financial management terms. As Drucker[12] has commented:

> And when it comes to finance, the "autonomous" subsidiary becomes a menace. The splintering of financial-management decisions is responsible in large measure for the poor performance of the U.S.-based multinationals during these past years of an over-valued dollar, when most of them lost both market standing and profitability—unnecessarily. We do know how to minimize the impacts of exchange-rate fluctuations on both sales and profits. Now that fluctuating exchange rates, subject to sudden wide swings and geared primarily to capital movements and to governmental decisions, have come to be the norm, localized financial management then requires taking financial operations away from all operating units, including the parent, and running them as systems operations — the way old hands at the game, such as Exxon and IBM, have for many years.

Pucik[13] has suggested that in order to properly evaluate a subsidiary's performance, a set of parallel accounts adjusted for the influence of financial manipulation may need to be maintained, or new measures of control developed, that are less susceptible to the influence of factors such as exchange-rate fluctuations, cash-flow and liquidity, and transfer pricing. Another alternative would be to evaluate a manager on the basis of subsidiary performance using achievement of long-range goals rather than measures such as profit or return on equity.

Much of the discussion in this chapter focuses on using financial data to evaluate how well an expatriate manager operates a foreign subsidiary. This results-oriented approach does not consider the way results are obtained and the behaviors used to obtain these results.[14] Concern with such issues as the Corrupt Foreign Practices Act may prompt an increased use of behavioral as well as results data to appraise the performance of the expatriate manager.

CONSTRAINTS ON STRATEGY-LEVEL APPRAISAL IN MNCs

In developing a suitable mix of long- and short-term objectives to be used as the framework of management appraisal on a strategic level, it is necessary to consider the implications of five major constraints that affect global strategy-level appraisal in MNCs.

Whole *versus* Part

To pursue a competitive global strategy, a MNC must necessarily focus on global performance rather than subsidiary or regional market performance. In the long run, the sum of short-term optimal sub-portfolio investments does not lead to optimal long-term performance for the MNC as a whole. The limitation of short-term local profit-maximization strategies can be seen when competitive pressure requires a multinational firm to operate and compete actively in markets where, if isolated from other markets, it would not compete. A typical case, described by Pucik,[15] is one in which a MNC enters a market where an international competitor is a dominant market leader. The objective of entering the market is to challenge the competitor's cash flow with aggressive pricing policies. The balance sheet of this particular subsidy might be continually in the red, but this strategy, by tying up the competitor's resources, may allow substantially higher returns in another market. The difficulties in quantifying such a global strategy in terms of the usual return-on-investment objectives are obvious.

Noncomparable Data

Frequently, the data obtained from subsidiaries may be neither interpretable nor reliable. For example:[16]

▸ Sales in Brazil may be skyrocketing, but there are reports that the Brazilian government may impose tough new exchange controls within a year, thus making it impossible for the MNC to repatriate profits. Does this mean that the MNC is performing effectively? Is the subsidiary performing effectively?

▸ Sales in Peru may be skyrocketing, but no one told the headquarters managers that under Peruvian accounting rules, sales on consignment are counted as firm sales. How should the headquarters accounting system handle these sales relative to sales from other subsidiaries, which do not consider sales on consignment as firm sales?

Physical measures of performance may be easier to interpret than in the examples, but difficulties may still arise. For example, notions of what constitutes adequate quality control checks can vary widely from one country to another, import tariffs can distort pricing schedules, a dock strike in one country can unexpectedly delay supply of necessary components to a manufacturing plant in another country, and local labor laws may require full employment at plants that are producing at below capacity. These factors can make objective appraisal of subsidiary performance problematic.

Volatility of the International Environment

The turbulence of the international environment requires that long-term goals be flexible in order to respond to potential market contingencies. An inflexible approach may mean that subsidiaries could be pursuing strategies that no longer fit the new environment. The interrelationship between the monitoring of relevant changes and the appraisal process is one important area in which corporate planning and human resource activities closely overlap. The volatility and fluctuations under which subsidiaries operate require precision tailoring of long-term goals to the specific situation in a given market. It is important to reconcile the tension between the need for universal appraisal standards with specific objectives in the subsidiaries.[17]

Separation by Time and Distance

Judgments concerning the congruence between long-term MNC strategy and activities in subsidiaries are further complicated by the physical distances involved, time-zone differences, the infrequency of contact between the corporate head-office staff and subsidiary management, and the cost of the reporting system. Developments in sophisticated worldwide communications systems such as Fax machines do not fully substitute for "face to face" contacts between subsidiary managers and MNC corporate staff. It is often necessary to meet personally with a manager to fully understand the problems that manager must deal with. For this reason, many MNC corporate HR managers spend a considerable amount of time traveling in order to meet HCN and TCN managers in foreign locations.

Variable Levels of Market Maturity

Without the supporting infrastructure of the parent company, the market development in foreign subsidiaries is generally slower and more difficult to achieve than at home, where established brands can support new products and new business areas can be cross-subsidized by other divisions. As a result, more time is needed to achieve results than is customary in a domestic market, and this fact ought to be recognized in the appraisal process. Further, variations in customs and work practices between the parent country and the foreign subsidiary must be considered. For example,

> One does not fire a Mexican manager because worker productivity is half the American average. In Mexico, that would mean that this manager is working at a level three or four times as high as the average Mexican industrial plant. Here we need relevant comparative data, not absolute numbers; our harassed Mexican manager has to live with Mexican constraints, not European or American ones, and these can be very different. The way we measure worker productivity is exactly the same, but the numbers come out differently because of that environmental difference.[18]

APPRAISAL OF HCN AND TCN EMPLOYEES

The discussion so far has omitted the issue of appraising the performance of the HCNs and the TCNs. This reflects the scarcity of research on the topic and the general lack of an acceptable way to address the situation.[19] In practice, U.S. MNCs have tried using the same appraisal form on HCNs and TCNs (and expatriates if they are not heading the subsidiary) as on their domestic employees without translation from English or the same form translated to the appropriate language. Both approaches have drawbacks. The use of English-worded forms may not be readily understood by HCN and TCN managers and their employees (nor do they easily apply to all jobs in all situations). Even when the forms are translated and then returned to the home office, they still may not be readily understood by the domestic staff.

The practice of performance appraisal itself confronts the issue of cultural applicability.[20] Performance appraisal in different nations can be interpreted as a signal of distrust or even an insult. As a consequence, MNCs have been hesitant about doing performance appraisals of their HCN and TCN employees.

SUMMARY

In this chapter we have discussed the MNC's need to determine if performance problems are due to management failure or to environmental constraints. To make this judgment, MNCs need to acquire accurate information. We discussed several types of information that can be gathered and the difficulties in gathering that information. A firm's communications requirements expand when it develops international markets because of the need for more information to properly evaluate subsidiary performance.[21]

In addition to the challenges in appraising the performance of each subsidiary manager, we discussed the challenges of comparing subsidiary managers in different countries. For example, it is difficult to compare the performance of a French subsidiary manager with that of a Singapore subsidiary manager because each manager works under quite different environmental conditions. It is equally as challenging to evaluate the performance of the employees (the majority of whom are HCNs) who work in the subsidiary.

We concluded that MNCs make broad assessments of how well their chosen strategies are working. They may anticipate certain monetary and real growth in markets in given countries, and in a general way their managers can evaluate overall financial results subject to all the difficulties noted in this chapter. The micro details about evaluating the performance of TCNs and HCNs, quality control, production norms, pay rates, supplier relations and much more can be analyzed with some of the same tools and techniques used by the parent company, allowing for some appreciation for local conditions and cultures. The need for appreciating and then adapting to the needs of the local conditions, however, cannot be overstated. This, of course, applies equally to all the international HRM activities we discuss in this book.

QUESTIONS

1. Discuss the major factors associated with appraisal of expatriate managerial performance.
2. What are some of the factors that influence appraisal of expatriate performance in subsidiary units?
3. Why is it important to distinguish between short-term and long-term objectives when assessing expatriate managerial performance?
4. In what ways would the role of a manager working in a less-developed country (LDC) differ from that of a manager in a developed western economy?
5. It is often claimed that U.S. managers are less skilled in cross-cultural interaction than are their European counterparts.* In your view, is this a fair comment?

FURTHER READING

1. C. P. Dredge, "Corporate Culture: The Challenge to Expatriate Managers and Multinational Corporations," in *Strategic Management of Multinational Corporations: The Essentials*, ed. H. V. Wortzel and L. H. Wortzel (New York: John Wiley, 1985).
2. J. M. Geringer, P. W. Beamish, and R. C. daCosta, "Diversification Strategy and Internationalization: Implications for MNE Performance," *Strategic Management Journal*, Vol. 10 (1989) pp. 109–119.
3. L. Leksell and U. Lindgren, "The Board of Directors in Foreign Subsidiaries," in *International Business Knowledge: Managing International Functions in the 1990s*, ed. W. A. Dymsza and R. G. Vambery (New York: Praeger, 1987).
4. P. Lorange, "Human Resource Management in Multinational Cooperative Ventures," *Human Resource Management*, Vol. 25, No. 1 (1986) pp. 133–148.
5. I. Torbiorn, "The Structure of Managerial Roles in Cross-Cultural Settings," *International Studies of Management and Organization*, Vol. 15, No. 1 (1985) pp. 52–74.

---

*For example, see Chapter 1 of V. Terpstra and K. David, *The Cultural Environment of International Business*, 2nd ed. (Cincinnati, Ohio: South-Western, 1985).

NOTES

1. This section is based in part on V. Pucik, "Strategic Human Resources Management in a Multinational Firm," in *Strategic Management of Multinational Corporations: The Essentials*, ed. H. V. Wortzel and L. H. Wortzel (New York: John Wiley, 1985), and is used with permission.

2. Ibid. p. 429.

3. This section is adapted from S. F. Slater and N. K. Napier, "Human Resource Competence as a Source of Competitive Advantage in Multinational Companies: Issues Affecting the Transfer of Distinctive Competence" (Working Paper, Boise State University, 1989). Used with permission. One of the dangers of performance appraisal is that, because the focus is so much on a particular individual, the teamwork aspect gets lost. In an international location, it is perhaps desirable to focus more on how the PCN has settled in and is operating as part of a team rather than as an individual at the possible detriment of the team.

4. Richard Hays, "Expatriate Selection: Insuring Success and Avoiding Failure," *Journal of International Business Studies*, Vol. 5, No. 1 (1974) pp. 25–37.

5. M. Conway, "Reducing Expatriate Failure Rates," *Personnel Administrator*, July 1984, pp. 31–37.

6. See I. Torbiorn, *Living Abroad: Personal Adjustment and Personnel Policy in the Overseas Setting* (New York: John Wiley, 1982).

7. See E. Dapsin, "Managing Expatriate Employees," *Management Review*, July 1985, pp. 47–49; W. Davidson, "Administrative Orientation and International Performance," *Journal of International Business Studies*, Fall 1984, pp. 11–23; G. Oddou and M. Mendenhall, "Expatriate Performance Appraisal: Problems and Solutions," under review at *Personnel*; and M. Mendenhall and G. Oddou, "The Overseas Assignment: A Practical Look," *Business Horizons*, September–October 1988, pp. 78–84.

8. See M. Harvey, "The Executive Family: An Overlooked Variable in International Assignments," *Columbia Journal of World Business*, Spring 1985, pp. 84–92; M. Harvey, "The Other Side of Foreign Assignments: Dealing with the Repatriation Dilemma," *Columbia Journal of World Business*, Vol. 17, No. 1 (1982) pp. 53–59; and Hays, "Expatriate Selection."

9. Hays, "Expatriate Selection."

10. Pucik, "Strategic Human Resource Management."

11. J. Garland and R. N. Farmer, *International Dimensions of Business Policy and Strategy* (Boston: PWS-KENT Publishing Co., 1986).

12. P. Drucker, "The Changing Multinational," *Wall Street Journal*, January 1, 1986, p. 12.

13. Pucik, "Strategic Human Resource Management."

14. R. W. Beatty, "Competitive Human Resource Advantages Through the Strategic Management of Performance," *Human Resource Planning*, Vol. 12, No. 3 (1989) pp. 179–194.

15. Ibid.

16. These examples are taken from Garland and Farmer, *International Dimensions*.

17. Pucik, "Strategic Human Resource Management."

18. Garland and Farmer, *International Dimensions*.

19. Personal conversations with Mark Mendenhall and Patrick Morgan, August 17, 1989.

20. N. J. Adler, *International Dimensions of Organizational Behavior* (Boston: PWS-KENT Publishing Company, 1986); S. Schneider, "National vs. Corporate Culture: Implications for Human Resource Management," *Human Resource Management*, Vol. 27 (1988) pp. 231–246; and G. P. Latham and N. K. Napier, "Chinese Human Resource Management Practices in Hong Kong and Singapore: An Exploratory Study," in *Research in Personnel and Human Resource Management*, Vol. 6, ed. G. Ferris, K. Rowland, and A. Nedd (Greenwich, Conn.: JAI, 1989).

21. Garland and Farmer, *International Dimensions*.

CHAPTER 5

▼

Training and Development

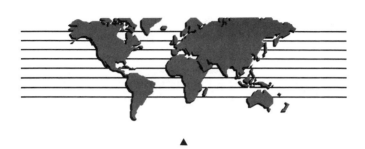

▲

To compete successfully in a global market, it is vital for MNCs to train PCNs, HCNs, and TCNs for service in overseas divisions. Once employees are chosen according to predetermined personal and professional characteristics, training and education in the culture of the host country and/or corporate headquarters is essential for successful performance in these positions. This chapter gives an overview of the many issues involved in international training and development.

THE SHIFT TO A GLOBAL MARKETPLACE

In the past, many MNCs tended to focus virtually all of their managerial development efforts on their PCN managers.[1] This approach to training and development matched a number of other assumptions about doing business internationally. For example, a MNC assumed it could continue to grow and prosper simply by providing the same kinds of goods and services it had in the past. Managers believed that replicating the staffing of the existing MNC in foreign locations — including maintaining the same perspectives, know-how, and skills at various levels — would keep the firm on track. Management development efforts were considered successful if they produced similarly qualified replacements for individual executives whenever they might be needed. The best and most efficient way to manage the MNC was believed to be a top-down, vertical chain of command. All major decisions were made at corporate headquarters by the CEO and senior managers (or, in the case of European countries, by the managing board). Line managers at lower organization levels were expected to manage the day-to-day operation of their assigned units in accordance with uniform company policies and directives, including detailed operating plans and budgets. They were not expected to concern themselves with any broader, longer-range issues.

Of course, not all companies were quite this rigid, but, in retrospect, many will admit they were. Today the situation is quite different for most MNCs. The business environment has become turbulent, fiercely competitive, and increasingly global in scope. Multinationals headquartered all over the world are increasingly recognizing the need for change and the need to manage their affairs in a much more flexible and dynamic way. Many MNCs are now focusing on what, when, and how to change rather than how to maintain the status quo. In order to maintain growth and profitability, MNCs have had to address the following issues:

▶ The need to determine in which businesses the MNC should operate and which competitive strategies must be followed to compete successfully in these businesses.

▶ The need to formulate detailed competitive strategies and develop viable implementation plans for these businesses.

▶ The need to be aware of and responsive to changing markets and changing technologies all over the world.

▶ The need to become more flexible and resilient in dealing with unexpected political, economic, and competitive challenges and opportunities.

Accomplishing these tasks requires a very different overall management system.[2] Characteristics of such a management system include the following:

▶ Major strategic decision-making responsibilities are distributed to teams of line executives in charge of business units throughout the organization (including those overseas). Each organization level deals with a different set of strategic issues and so adds value in a different way. An interaction dialogue between the various parts and levels of the organization enables managers to reach agreement on appropriate strategies and to allocate available resources.

▶ Information gathering and information sharing become integral parts of each line manager's job, whether at home or abroad.

▶ There is recognition of local needs and the need to provide training, development, and promotion opportunities for HCNs and TCNs as well as PCNs.

▶ Close teamwork is needed in planning and smoothly implementing strategically necessary change without undermining the viability of ongoing operations.

The demands of managing business internationally call for different perspectives and skills and a much greater tolerance for ambiguity and uncertainty. These requirements must be taken into account when planning management training and development programs for MNCs, regardless of whether these programs take place in the home country or abroad.

LINKING STRATEGY AND STRUCTURE WITH INTERNATIONAL TRAINING AND DEVELOPMENT

The type of international operation is a key consideration in planning and establishing international training and development needs in a MNC. Each of the following four types of operations calls for different international training and development needs. (These types correspond roughly to the stages of development introduced in Chapter 2.)

Limited Relationships

The first type of operation is the MNC with international sales through export offices, sales representatives, joint ventures, or distributor relationships. Businesses in this category generally limit their management development efforts to their own managers, but some also offer to help their partners' managers. Furthermore, if they see these export arrangements as temporary — as stepping stones to country businesses or mother-daughter organizations — they may also provide some business management training and development to the sales representatives, key liaison executives, or even heads of various partner organizations. Assuming these executives have all lived in the particular country, they are high-potential candidates for future management positions in the MNC. They already know the territory and the business, and they need opportunities to develop their strategic leadership skills and their general operating management skills.

Subsidiaries

The second type of operation is the firm with national subsidiaries. Because of the current emphasis on the management of businesses, subsidiaries are now likely to be represented on several lines of business strategy teams. Sometimes it is necessary to have a PCN head up a country subsidiary at first, but there is general agreement that over time the entire management team should be from the host country. Training and development opportunities need to be provided to local managers to enable them to learn how the subsidiary operates and to develop the skills required to fulfill their managerial roles.

If the MNC decides to establish regional businesses, the managers from the various subsidiaries need to meet with each other to discuss recent developments and mutual problems, to share ideas and information and possible solution suggestions, and to begin to understand the reasons for their differing points of view. Some MNCs provide for temporary transfers between subsidiaries as a way of addressing these problems.

Regional Businesses

The third type of operation is the firm with regional businesses. If the senior managers have lived in different countries within the region, there should be an awareness of the cultural and geographic differences that must be balanced in arriving at overall strategies and business plans for the region. There are a number of training and development issues involved in operating regional businesses. First, future PCN regional managers require several developmental assignments overseas before they are able to take up senior positions at regional headquarters. Second, host- and third-country nationals also require developmental assignments and training in strategic leadership skills and financial analysis.

In the future, it is likely that executives who have headed major regional businesses will be prime candidates to become CEOs of those same businesses on a global scale. To prepare them for future assignments and to ensure that current global business strategies appropriately balance the interests of all regions, leading-edge companies are including their regional business leaders as members of the top management teams running each of their global businesses.

Global Businesses

The final type of operation is the MNC that is a world-class company with several global businesses. Such firms report that management development programs need to emphasize worldwide information sharing on economic, social, political, technological, and market trends and to focus on building teamwork across related business lines as well as across functional and country-regional lines.

It is important to note that in practice this rather simple progression for categorizing international business development options and international management development options is more complex than it seems. The provision of relevant international training and development for managers will always be a challenging task. As Pucik[3] has noted, "Probably the most formidable task recently facing many multinational firms is the development of a cadre of managers and executives who have an understanding of the global market environment deep enough to enable them to survive and come out ahead." Part of the challenge lies in the fact that many MNCs have in the past paid too little attention to the issue of international training and development. Many MNCs traditionally relied on developing a cadre of career international management employees who moved from one international assignment to the next. (This system is often referred to as the "colonial model" because many European MNCs followed this pattern in the first half of this century.) Many MNCs are now recognizing that they need to provide international experience to many levels of managers (regardless of nationality) and not just to a small cadre of PCNs. Thus, many MNCs are now developing larger pools of employees with international experience through increasing use of short-term developmental assignments ranging from a few months to several years.

Multinational corporations are now providing training and development opportunities for their TCN and HCN employees as well. This training is necessary in order to help develop a true cadre of international managers and to be able to localize products and services as needed. It is also necessary in order to motivate TCN and HCN employees. Many MNCs now try to balance the extent and level of involvement of PCNs in foreign operations. For example, Kodak often places U.S. PCNs in the number two or number three positions in overseas operations, leaving the chief executive job for a HCN. This kind of staffing means that MNCs must place more emphasis on the training of HCN and TCN managers, especially critical in countries where trained people are in short supply. The value of well-trained HCNs is emphasized by a senior HR manager of a large MNC in the chemical industry:[4]

> In Latin America, finding qualified trained people at all levels to staff the organization is a major challenge. The talent pool is much thinner in Latin America and many times we have to lower our hiring standards because we can't find people. This in turn generates a much greater need to train in-house after we hire. Also, after we develop good people we have to work harder at keeping them. For example, we develop a good person to be a treasurer and believe they will be the next financial director. Before the opening occurs another company hires them as financial director because this person is the best candidate they can find. Also, local companies want to hire people from multinational companies.

Multinationals must address the growing need for international training and development and deal with controversial questions concerning how many employees will be trained, what the overall purpose of the training is, and who should receive training (PCNs, HCNs, and/or TCNs). In reality, most MNCs continue to direct most of their training and development resources to PCNs.

TRAINING AND DEVELOPMENT FOR EXPATRIATE MANAGERS

Although they are aware of the reality of the "global village" and the imperative of successfully competing worldwide, many U.S. MNC expatriates are not prepared for their assignments. For example, studies have found that between 16 and 40 percent of all American managers sent on foreign assignments return prematurely because of poor performance or because of the inability to adjust to the foreign environment.[5] Other studies have found that negotiations between businessmen of different cultures often fail because of problems related to cross-cultural differences.[6] The costs of these failed cross-cultural interactions and failed expatriate assignments are high. For a firm with hundreds of expatriate employees worldwide, the costs can easily reach into the millions of dollars. Copeland and Griggs have estimated that the direct costs of failed expatriate assignments is over $2 billion a year, and this does not include unmeasured losses such as damaged corporate reputations or lost business opportunities.[7]

Cross-cultural training has long been advocated as a means of facilitating effective cross-cultural interactions,[8] yet most firms do not use cross-cultural training. For example, only 30 percent of managers being sent on one- to five-year expatriate assignments receive training before their departure.[9] Although various reasons have been cited by business organizations for the low use of cross-cultural training, the main reason seems to be that top management just doesn't believe the training is necessary or effective.[10]

This situation needs to be changed. Training and development of expatriates should begin where selection ends. The basic aspects of expatriate development include the following:

▸ development of expatriates before, during, and after foreign assignment
▸ orientation and training of expatriate families before, during, and after foreign assignments
▸ development of the headquarters staff responsible for the planning, organization, and control of overseas operations

In designing international training and development for their expatriates, MNCs need to recognize the importance of multiple home-country and host-country role relationships, shown in Figure 5–1. In addition, international training and development programs need to recognize the importance of bringing about attitudinal and behavioral changes in the expatriates and their families. The major issues that need to be addressed in expatriate training and development are discussed in the following pages and summarized in Figure 5–2.

Once an employee has been selected for an expatriate position, cross-cultural training becomes the next critical step in attempting to ensure the expatriate's effectiveness and success abroad. (This training is in addition, of course, to the task-specific knowledge necessary for the position.) Depending on the assigned country, the employee and his or her family may be confronted with a culture markedly different from their

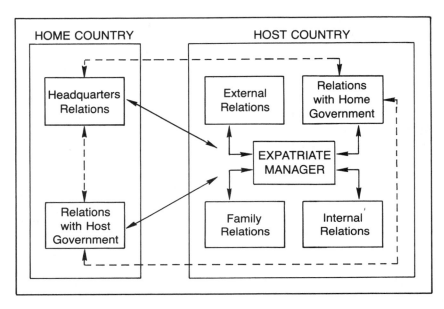

FIGURE 5–1 Major Relations Between the Expatriate Manager and Other Parties Interested in International Business
SOURCE: A. Rahim. "A Model for Developing Key Expatriate Executives," *Personnel Journal*, April 1983, p. 313.

own. These contrasts can extend beyond the language barrier and encompass aspects of social life, political climate, and religious differences.[11]

Studies[12] indicate that there are three areas that contribute to a smooth transition to a foreign post: cultural training, language instruction, and assistance with practical, day-to-day matters. The first two phases necessarily begin prior to the international assignment. The last category, practical assistance, begins once the employee arrives in the host country.

Cultural Training

To be effective, the expatriate employee must adapt to and not feel isolated from the host country. A cultural training program can be extremely beneficial. The potential benefits of cultural or cross-cultural

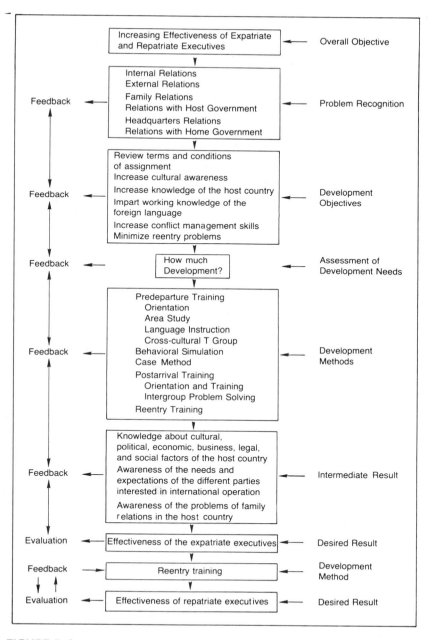

FIGURE 5-2 A Model for the Development of Multinational Management
SOURCE: A. Rahim. "A Model for Developing Key Expatriate Executives," *Personnel Journal*, April 1983, p. 313.

training are widely acknowledged, yet this type of training is not offered by most U.S. MNCs.[13]

Cultural training seeks to foster an appreciation of the host country's culture so that expatriates can behave accordingly. Sieveking, Anchor, and Marston[14] cite the culture of the Middle East to emphasize this point. In that region, emphasis is placed on personal relationships, trust, and respect in business dealings. Coupled with this is an overriding emphasis on religion that permeates almost every aspect of life. Without an understanding (or at least an acceptance) of the host-country culture in such a situation, the expatriate is likely to face considerable difficulty during the international assignment. As discussed in Chapter 4, flexibility appears to be an important characteristic for the expatriate.

Baliga and Baker[15] suggest that the expatriate receive training concentrated in the assigned region's culture, history, politics, economy, religion, and social and business practices. They advocate a training program focused on a particular location as opposed to one in which employees are made aware of broad differences in cultures and encouraged merely to be open to them. Only with precise knowledge of the varied components of their host culture can the expatriate and family grasp how and why people behave and react as they do. According to Harris,[16] it is also important to include the family in cultural training programs. "In the past, the family has not received an appropriate amount of attention," he has noted. "The biggest problem for Americans overseas is not technical know-how, rather it is some kind of spousal and/or child problem."

Because of the skills and complexities involved, many MNCs employ specialists such as Moran, Stahl & Boyer in the United States or the Center for International Briefing (known as Farnham Castle) in Britain to conduct cultural training programs.[17] These training programs enable the employee, spouse, and children to become more flexible and adaptive by exposing participants to new information and experiences. In addition to these specialists, there are "how-to" books such as Copeland and Griggs's *Going International*.[18] Recent research suggests that the most effective cultural training programs use a variety of source material. For example, an interesting paper by Earley[19] suggests that MNCs should use both documentary and interpersonal methods to prepare managers for intercultural assignments.

Some European MNCs, such as Philips, have incorporated cultural training into their career planning process. For example, employees may be posted to an overseas subsidiary for three or four years to fulfill both operational and management development objectives. Some U.S. MNCs such as Hercules Incorporated, Ford, Dow Chemical, Monsanto, Westinghouse, and General Electric have successfully applied a similar approach to training and development. Such an approach is less common with U.S. MNCs, however, and this may be one reason for the reported high failure rate for U.S. expatriates (see Chapter 3).

One developmental technique useful for orienting international employees is to send them on a preliminary trip to the host country.[20] A well-planned trip overseas for the candidate and spouse provides a preview that allows them to assess their suitability for and interest in the assignment. Such a trip also serves to introduce expatriate candidates to business outside their own country and helps encourage more informed predeparture preparation.

Effective and comprehensive cultural training programs can ease transition and help to develop productive expatriates. They can also prevent mistakes such as that of the highly paid expatriate who brought two miniature bottles of brandy with him into Qatar (a Muslim country in the Middle East), was discovered by customs, and was promptly deported, causing his firm to be "disinvited" and ordered never to return.

Language Training

Language training is a seemingly obvious orientation needed for a successful and productive experience abroad and should form part of any long-term management development program for future global executives.[21] As noted in Chapter 3, there is general recognition that English is the language of world business, and it is quite possible to conduct routine operations around the world using English only, but an exclusive reliance on English diminishes the incentive to develop the linguistic capacity of the MNC and the ability to process foreign-language data in a timely manner.

It is also important to note that multilingual employees of MNCs from non–English-speaking countries are able to monitor the activities of their English-speaking competitors by reading English-language publications (the voluminous business press in an open society such as the United States frequently gives detailed accounts of the strategic plans of large companies). For example, many engineers and managers in Japanese computer companies have a sufficient command of English to enable them to understand English-language trade journals and conference presentations, often sources of valuable business intelligence. In contrast, their English-speaking counterparts employ only a handful of engineers capable of following Japanese-language materials and of making the proper inference between publicly available information and its underlying strategic significance — a task that an outside translation service is not equipped to handle.

It appears that the importance of language training is not appreciated by many MNCs. A study by Baker of seventy-four executives of MNCs found that only twenty-three of them felt that knowledge of foreign languages was necessary for conducting business abroad.[22] Those firms offering language training believed that it improved the effectiveness of employees and enabled them to relate more easily to a foreign culture, which in turn fostered a better image of the MNC in the host country. Those who responded that knowledge of a foreign language was not necessary most frequently cited the fact that English was the basis for conducting company business, regardless of the country in question. Baker found a markedly different attitude among those who were assigned to non–English-speaking countries.[23] Of these respondents, more than 36 percent felt that knowledge of the local language was important, and 32 percent of the companies surveyed offered language training. Most did not offer in-house training but instead sent employees to language-learning facilities such as Alliance Française, the Goethe Institute, Berlitz, and local university programs. In-house language training is less frequently used because of the relatively high cost per participant.

Clearly, the ability to speak a foreign language can improve the expatriate's effectiveness and negotiating ability. As Baliga and Baker[24] point out, it can improve managers' access to information regarding the host country's economy, government, and market. In addition, expatriates can more easily fit into their adapted country socially whether or not English is spoken by foreign nationals. As we noted in Chapter 3, Mendenhall and Oddou[25] make the important point that willingness to communicate does not refer to level of fluency in a foreign language but rather the expatriate's confidence and willingness to use the host culture's language.

Practical Training

Practical assistance makes an important contribution toward the adaptation of the expatriate and his or her family to their new environment. Being left to fend for themselves would most likely result in a negative response toward the host country's culture. Lanier[26] states that the MNC needs to assist the expatriate family in establishing a new support network. The sooner a pattern of day-to-day life involving friends, banks, shopping, laundry, transportation, and so on is established, the better the prospects are that the expatriates will adapt successfully. A useful method of adaptation involves interaction between the expatriate's family and other established expatriate families. These encounters allow the exchange of information facilitating adaptation and serve to build a stable network of relationships for the expatriate's family. If fluency in the host-country language is important for successful adaptation, further language training for the expatriate and family should occur after arrival. Orientation programs and local language programs are normally organized by the personnel staff in the host country. Adaptation and assimilation, however, go in both directions:

> In order to help close the cultural gap, it is not always enough to just take the expat and family and explain what the local culture/language is all about. It is equally important to take the local employees and explain to them who are these "gringos" and why are they so strange. This helps with mutual assimilation.[27]

Contingency Approaches to Expatriate Training

Because not all expatriate assignments are the same, expatriate training is likely to vary. To understand possible variations in expatriate training, Tung[28] proposed a contingency framework for deciding the nature and level of rigor of training. She argued that the two determining factors were the degree of interaction required in the host culture and the similarity between the individual's native culture and the new culture. The related training elements involved the content of the training and the rigor of the training. Essentially, Tung argued that if the expected interaction between the individual and members of the host culture was low and the degree of dissimilarity between the individual's native culture and the host culture was low, then the content of the training should focus on task- and job-related issues rather than culture-related issues, and the level of rigor necessary for effective training should be relatively low. If there was a high level of expected interaction with host nationals and a large dissimilarity between the cultures, then the content of the training should focus on the new culture and on cross-cultural skill development as well as on the new task, and the level of rigor for such training should be moderate to high.

This model does specify some criteria (degree of expected interaction and cultural similarity) for making training method decisions, but the conclusions the model allows the user to make are fairly general. The model helps the user determine when to emphasize task issues and when to emphasize culture learning along with skill development and task issues, but it does not help the user determine which specific training methods to use or what might constitute more or less rigorous training.

A more recent model presented by Mendenhall and Oddou and Mendenhall, Dunbar, and Oddou in some ways moves beyond Tung's model and provides more specific guidelines.[29] Like Tung, Mendenhall, Dunbar, and Oddou acknowledge the importance of degree of expected interaction and similarity between the native and host cultures in determining the cross-cultural training method. In addition, they propose three key elements related to training. The first is the training method Based on cross-cultural training typologies such as the one by Landis and Brislin,[30] Mendenhall, Dunbar, and Oddou propose a three-part classification system of training methods that essentially correspond to low, medium, and high levels of rigor. The first group of methods, termed *information-giving approaches*, is similar to Landis and Brislin's typologies of factual briefing, attribution training, and culture awareness and includes some specific methods such as area and cultural briefings or informative films and books. This group of approaches has a relatively low level of rigor.

The second group of methods, termed *affective approaches*, is similar to Landis and Brislin's cognitive-behavioral modification category. It includes such specific methods as culture assimilator training, critical incidents, role-plays, and case studies. This group of approaches has a moderate level of rigor.

The third group of methods, termed *immersion approaches*, is similar to Landis and Brislin's experiential and interaction training categories. This group includes such training methods as assessment centers, field experiences, and simulations. This group has the highest level of rigor.

Using the Mendenhall, Dunbar, and Oddou model, if the expected level of interaction is low and the degree of similarity between the individual's native culture and the host culture is high, the length of the training should probably be less than a week and methods such as area or cultural briefings via lectures, movies, or books would provide the appropriate level of training rigor. On the other hand, if the individual is going overseas for a period of two to twelve months and is expected to have some interaction with members of the host culture, the level of training rigor should be higher and its length longer (one to four weeks). In addition to the information-giving approaches, training methods such as culture assimilators and role-plays may be appropriate.

If the individual is going to a fairly novel and different host culture and the expected degree of interaction is high, the level of cross-cultural training rigor should be high and training should last as long as two months. In addition to the less rigorous methods already discussed, sensitivity training, field experiences, and intercultural experiential workshops may be appropriate training methods in this situation. Ronen's model of these high-level methods and their techniques and purposes is shown in Exhibit 5-1. Ronen[31] suggests a rather novel technique, the

EXHIBIT 5-1 *Training Techniques*

Method	*Technique*	*Purpose*
Didactic-Informational Training	▸ Lectures ▸ Reading material ▸ Videotapes ▸ Movies	Area studies, company operation, parent-country institutions
Intercultural Experiential Workshops	▸ Cultural assimilators ▸ Simulations ▸ Role playing	Culture-general, culture-specific negotiation skills; reduce ethnocentrism
Sensitivity Training	▸ Communication workshops ▸ T groups ▸ Outward-Bound trips	Self-awareness, communication style, empathy, listening skills, nonjudgmentalism
Field Experiences	▸ Meeting with ex-IAs ▸ Minicultures ▸ Host-family surrogate	Customs, values, beliefs, nonverbal behavior, religion
Language Skills	▸ Classes ▸ Cassettes	Interpersonal communication, job requirements, survival necessities

SOURCE: S. Ronen, "Training the International Assignee," in *Training and Career Development*, ed. I. Goldstein (San Francisco: Jossey-Bass, 1989), p. 430. Used by permission.

host-family surrogate, as a field experience. Used when the cross-cultural training rigor should be quite high, this technique places the designated expatriate and family in a domestically located family of the nationality to which they are assigned. The family is paid by the MNC to help prepare the expatriate and family for the international assignment.

The model presented by Mendenhall, Dunbar, and Oddou seems to be a significant improvement over the more general model offered by Tung. It provides a grouping of specific methods by level of rigor and also discusses the duration of training relative to the criteria of interaction and culture similarity. Despite these important improvements, the model tells us little about the training and learning processes and, therefore, why the particular determinations are made. In addition, the content of the training seems to be primarily "cultural" in nature, with little integration of the individual's new tasks and the new host culture. Finally, although both models make intuitive sense, the theoretical grounding is never made explicit, and, therefore, in the absence of empirical data to support the models, it is difficult to evaluate their soundness for use and success in the real world.

More recently, Black and Mendenhall have developed a much more extensive theoretically based model using Bandura's Social Learning Theory.[32] Although it is too early for empirical research on their propositions, they appear to offer a useful way to determine the appropriate content and method of expatriate training programs and to evaluate their success.

INTERNATIONAL TRAINING
AND DEVELOPMENT FOR HCNs AND TCNs

The bulk of this chapter has so far focused on the expatriate, or PCN. It is important that MNCs also consider the training and development needs of their HCN and TCN employees. Such training may involve development of managerial skills or introduction to the MNC's corporate culture. Technical training for lower-level local employees is generally provided by the country subsidiary rather than corporate headquarters.

One of the main aims of managerial training for HCNs and TCNs is to teach managers how to lead, motivate, and develop employees in their own countries. As many MNCs are discovering, a quality enhancement approach requires not just making sure that employees have the skills, but also making sure that managers have good people management skills. This generally means that HCN and TCN managers need to participate more in the company. In many cases, this means changing their entire way of operating. As one U.S. respondent to the Schuler and Dowling survey of ASPA/I members noted:[33]

> Implementing a quality improvement process, requiring a new role of managers, is tough enough in the U.S., but management labor "class" distinctions which are very prevalent in the U.K., France, and Germany, and seem almost sanctioned, *de facto*, in labor law make this task very difficult.

Thus, one of the traps that should be avoided is to try to export home-country training and development programs to other countries for local employees without any recognition that the training must be culturally adapted to meet local conditions. Many MNCs develop their HCN and TCN employees by bringing them to corporate headquarters. This experience exposes HCNs and TCNs to the headquarters corporate culture and assists them in developing a corporate perspective rather than simply reflecting their own local interests.[34] This type of training and development can be a very effective and necessary part of successfully operating a truly global firm. Training HCNs and TCNs can also be done for the purpose of developing the global management teams described at the beginning of this chapter. Through rotational experiences and international meetings, bonds of friendship can develop between individuals from all parts of the globe. These bonds can be used in the future to build truly global teams.

EMERGING ISSUES IN INTERNATIONAL TRAINING AND DEVELOPMENT

Two important emerging issues are the dual-career dilemma and the training of foreign managers (HCNs and TCNs) transferred to work in the parent country of the MNC.

Dual Careers

The dual-career dilemma is becoming more important, particularly in the U.S. in the financial services industry, which has a relatively high number of female managers who are increasingly being sent overseas on a short-term basis. In the past, working spouses were less common, generally female, and prepared to follow their partner's career transfers.[35] This past situation is reflected in the use of terms such as "the trailing spouse" to refer to the housebound female who accompanied her husband.

A number of issues need to be resolved when one member of a dual-career couple is offered the opportunity of an international assignment:

▸ Should the spouse disrupt his/her career to follow a partner's international assignment?

▸ If the spouse decides to follow his/her partner, will a job be available in the foreign location? Will he/she be able to obtain a work visa? In the case of female spouses, does the foreign country allow females to be employed? (The prohibition of female employment is common in many Middle East countries.)

▸ What responsibilities should the MNC take in assisting spouses to obtain employment?

MNCs need to recognize that dual-career problems can seriously affect career development plans for their international employees.

Foreign Managers

Establishing truly global operations means having a cadre of international managers (PCNs, HCNs, and TCNs) who are available to go anywhere in the world. To develop this cadre of managers, MNCs need to provide training for HCNs and TCNs in the parent country. This issue is of particular concern to U.S. MNCs, who are increasingly having to deal with the problem of helping HCNs and TCNs adjust to working in the United States. Just as Americans doing business abroad must grapple with unfamiliar social and commercial practices, so, too, must European, Asian and Latin American managers who are coming in growing numbers to work in the United States. To lessen the culture shock, many companies are relying on consultants to provide books, movies, and special programs that educate foreign employees about corporate life in the United States. Some have taken the language instruction, tax advice, and orientation techniques used when Americans are sent abroad and modified them to accommodate foreigners transferred to the United States. Others are trying a sort of buddy system, pairing foreign newcomers with American managers.[36]

Some MNCs are offering training and development programs that teach foreign managers how to motivate Americans and how to conduct performance appraisal interviews:

> Some of the programs designed to speed acculturation are intensive and emotionally strenuous. One U.S. manufacturer has retained trainers to stage role-playing sessions for its Japanese managers, some of whom have had special difficulty with American bluntness. During one of these, in which a Japanese manager was told to criticize an American employee's performance, "it took five runs of the same situation until he was direct enough that the American could realize he was being criticized," says Gary Wedersphan, a director of the international division of Moran, Stahl & Boyer, the consulting firm that conducted the sessions.[37]

SUMMARY

This chapter has shown that development of an internationally focused training and development program cannot be accomplished effectively without close coordination of developmental activities with the corporate strategic objectives. Issues include the nature and extent of current and future product markets, whether the MNC will have sufficient trained personnel to compete effectively in these product markets, and the need to develop an international cadre of managers who can manage international businesses in a variety of operating arrangements (joint ventures, subsidiaries, regional businesses, and so on). Analysis of these issues should provide parameters for HR staff, to enable them to plan training and developmental activities that are congruent with the MNC's strategic objectives. International training and development activities that are unrelated to overall strategic objectives are likely to be ineffective. Similarly, a MNC's strategic plan that does not consider appropriate human resource training and development programs is likely to be unsustainable.

QUESTIONS

1. Compare and contrast the traditional management system of MNCs to the management approaches used today in many global companies.
2. What are some of the challenges faced in training expatriate managers?

3. Identify the key aspects of a successful expatriate training and development program.
4. Why are dual-career couples and training of foreign managers two crucial issues in international training and development?
5. What are the issues and challenges MNCs face in developing a cadre of global managers?

FURTHER READING

1. R. Andre, "The Effects of Multinational Business Training: A Replication of INSEAD Research in an Institution in the United States," *Management International Review*, March 1985, pp. 4–15.
2. J. C. Baker, "Company Policies and Executives' Wives Abroad," *Industrial Relations*, October 1976, pp. 343–348.
3. C. Edinger, "Should You Work for a Foreigner?" *Fortune*, August 1, 1988, pp. 123–134.
4. C. Gould, "A Checklist for Accepting a Job Abroad," *New York Times*, July 17, 1988, p. 9.
5. J. Kepler, et al. *Americans Abroad: A Handbook for Living and Working Overseas.* New York: Praeger, 1983.
6. G. Latham, "Human Resource Training and Development," *Annual Review of Psychology*, Vol. 39 (1988) pp. 545–582.
7. R. Nath, "Role of Culture in Cross-Cultural and Organizational Research," *Advances in International Comparative Management*, 1986, pp. 249–267.
8. J. Onto, "Preparing Managers for International Careers: A Strategic Perspective," *Human Resource Management Australia*, Vol. 25, No. 3 (1987) pp. 22–33.
9. R. S. Savich and W. Rodgers, "Assignments Overseas: Easing the Transition Before and After," *Personnel*, August 1988, pp. 44–48.
10. N. Shahzad, "The American Expatriate Manager," *Personnel Administrator*, July 1984, pp. 23–30.

NOTES

1. This discussion of the historical development of international business is adapted from R. Shaeffer, "Managing International Business Growth and International Management Development," *Human Resource Planning*, March 1989, pp. 29–36.

2. J. E. Harris, "Moving Managers Internationally: The Care and Feeding of Expatriates," *Human Resource Planning*, March 1989, pp. 49–54.

3. This section is adapted from V. Pucik, "Strategic Human Resource Management in a Multinational Firm," in *Strategic Management of Multinational Corporations: The Essentials*, ed. H. V. Wortzel and L. H. Wortzel (New York: John Wiley, 1985). Used by permission.

4. R. S. Schuler and P. J. Dowling, "Survey of ASPA/I Members" (Stern School of Business, New York University, 1988).

5. J. C. Baker and J. M. Ivancevich, "The Assignment of American Executives Abroad: Systematic, Haphazard, or Chaotic?" *California Management Review*, Vol. 13 (1971) pp. 39–44; J. S. Black, "Work Role Transitions: A Study of American Expatriate Managers in Japan," *Journal of International Business Studies*, Vol. 19 (1988) pp. 277–294; E. Dunbar and M. Ehrlich, "International Practices, Selection, Training, and Managing the International Staff: A Survey Report" (The Project on International Human Resource, Columbia University Teachers College, 1986); R. Tung, "Selecting and Training of Personnel for Overseas Assignments, *Columbia Journal of World Business*, Vol. 16 (1981) pp. 68–78; M. Harvey, "Repatriation of Corporate Executives: An Empirical Study," *Journal of International Business Studies* (Spring 1989); G. Oddou and M. Mendenhall, "The Career Impact of an Overseas Assignment" (Paper presented at the Career Issues in International Management Symposium, Academy of Management, Washington, D.C., August 15, 1989); Korn/Ferry International, "A Study of Repatriation of the American International Executive" (New York, 1989); H. Schwind, "The State of the Art in Cross-Cultural Management Training," in *International Human Resource Development Annual, Volume 1*, ed. Robert Doktor (Alexandria, Va.: ASTD, 1985), pp. 7–15.

6. J. Graham, "The Influence of Culture on the Process of Business Negotiations: An Exploratory Study," *Journal of International Business Studies*, Spring 1984, pp. 81–95; and R. Tung, *Key to Japan's Economic Strength: Human Power* (Lexington, MA: Lexington Books, 1984).

7. L. Copeland and L. Griggs, *Going International* (New York: Random House, 1985).

8. R. W. Brislin, *Cross-Cultural Encounters* (New York: Pergamon Press, 1981); D. Landis and R. Brislin, *Handbook on Intercultural Training, Vol. 1* (New York: Pergamon Press, 1983); and M. Mendenhall, E. Dunbar, and G. Oddou, "Expatriate Selection, Training, and Career-Pathing: A Review and Critique," *Human Resource Management*, Vol. 26 (1987) pp. 331–345.

9. "Expatriation/Repatriation Survey" (Runzheimer Executive Report No. 31, Rochester, Wisc., 1984).

10. M. Mendenhall and G. Oddou, "The Dimensions of Expatriate Acculturation," *Academy of Management Review*, Vol. 10 (1985) pp. 39–47;

Schwind, "The State of the Art"; and Y. Zeira, "Overlooked Personnel Problems in Multinational Corporations," *Columbia Journal of World Business*, Vol. 10, No. 2 (1975) pp. 96–103.

11. This section is adapted from N. Napier, M. Taylor, and S. Slater, "Human Resource Competence as a Source of Competitive Advantages in Multinational Companies: Issues Affecting the Transfer of Human Resource Management Competence" (Working Paper, Boise State University, 1988).

12. M. Mendenhall and G. Oddou, "Acculturation Profiles of Expatriate Managers: Implications for Cross-cultural Training Programs," *Columbia Journal of World Business* (Winter 1986) pp. 73–79. R. W. Brislin, *Cross Cultural Encounters;* and D. Landis and R. W. Brislin, *Handbook on Intercultural Training.*

13. J. S. Black and M. Mendenhall, "Cross-Cultural Training Effectiveness: A Review and a Theoretical Framework for Future Research," *Academy of Management Review,* in press.

14. N. Sieveking, B. Anchor, and R. Marston, "Selecting and Preparing Expatriate Employees," *Personnel Journal,* March 1981, pp. 197–202. See also N. Sieveking and R. Marston, "Critical Selection and Orientation of Expatriates," *Personnel Administrator,* April 1978, pp. 20–23.

15. G. Baliga and J. C. Baker, "Multinational Corporate Policies for Expatriate Managers: Selection, Training, and Evaluation," *Advanced Management Journal,* Autumn 1985, pp. 31–38.

16. Harris, "Moving Managers Internationally."

17. For more detailed information on organizations that specialize in international training, see Chapter 2, "Training Institutes for International Assignments," in R. L. Tung, *The New Expatriates: Managing Human Resources Abroad* (Cambridge, Mass.: Ballinger, 1988).

18. Copeland and Griggs, *Going International.*

19. P. Earley, "International Training for Managers: A Comparison of Documentary and Interpersonal Methods," *Academy of Management Journal,* Vol. 30 (1987) pp. 685–698.

20. J. Blue and U. Haynes, "Preparation for the Overseas Assignment," *Business Horizons,* June 1977, pp. 61–67.

21. This section is adapted from V. Pucik, "Strategic Human Resource Management."

22. J. C. Baker, "Foreign Language and Departure Training in U.S. Multinational Firms," *Personnel Administrator,* July 1984, pp. 68–70.

23. Ibid.

24. Baliga and Baker, "Multinational Corporate Policies."

25. Mendenhall and Oddou, "Dimensions of Expatriate Acculturation."

26. A. Lanier, "Selecting and Preparing Personnel for Overseas Transfers," *Personnel Journal*, March 1979, pp. 160–163.

27. Personal communication with Patrick Morgan, August 1989.

28. This section on contingency is adapted from J. S. Black and M. Mendenhall (citing Tung). "Selecting Cross-Cultural Training Methods: A Practical Yet Theory-Based Approach" (Working Paper, Amos Tuck School of Business, Dartmouth College, 1990; under review at *Human Resource Management*).

29. M. Mendenhall and G. Oddou, "Acculturation Profiles of Expatriate Managers: Implications for Cross-Cultural Training Programs," *Columbia Journal of World Business*, Vol. 21 (1986) pp. 73–79; and Mendenhall, Dunbar, and Oddou, "Expatriate Selection, Training and Career-Pathing."

30. Landis and Brislin, *Handbook on Intercultural Training*.

31. S. Ronen, "Training an International Assignee," in *Training and Career Development*, ed. I. Goldstein (San Francisco: Jossey-Bass, 1990).

32. Black and Mendenhall, "Cross-Cultural Training Effectiveness;" and A. Bandura, *Social Learning Theory* (Englewood Cliffs, N.J.: Prentice-Hall, 1977).

33. Schuler and Dowling, "Survey of ASPA/I Members."

34. A number of writers have also made the point that this form of developmental transfer can also function as a coordination and control strategy. See A. Edstrom and J. Galbraith, "Transfer of Managers as a Coordination and Control Strategy in Multinational Organizations," *Administrative Science Quarterly*, Vol. 22 (1977) pp. 248–263; and C. K. Prahalad and Y. L. Doz, "An Approach to Strategic Control in MNCs," *Sloan Management Review*, Vol. 22, No. 4 (1981) pp. 5–13.

35. For a review of the literature on dual careers, see Chapter 9, "A Portable Life: The Expatriate Spouse," in N. J. Adler, *International Dimensions of Organizational Behavior* (Boston: PWS-KENT Publishing Co., 1986).

36. This section is based on A. Bennett, "American Culture is Often a Puzzle for Foreign Managers in the U.S.," *Wall Street Journal*, February 12, 1988, p. 33.

37. Ibid.

CHAPTER 6

▼

Compensation

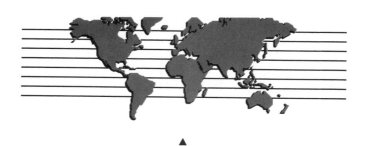

▲

To successfully manage international compensation and benefits requires knowledge of the laws, customs, environment, and employment practices of many foreign countries; familiarity with currency relationships and the effect of inflation on compensation; and an understanding of why special allowances must be supplied and which allowances are necessary in what countries — all within the context of shifting political, economic, and social conditions.

Human resource managers spend a great deal of time developing effective compensation and benefit programs for international employees because these highly skilled, educated professionals and managers are high-cost employees. American PCNs have become so expensive, in fact, that many American MNCs have repatriated all but their most essential overseas employees.[1] The Schuler and Dowling survey of ASPA/I members[2] found that the most common challenge mentioned about PCN compensation was managing the expense. One respondent noted, "We have operated for many years overseas. The weak dollar at the moment makes it very expensive to have U.S. PCNs overseas. Housing becomes exorbitant in strong currency countries." Nonetheless, there will always be a core group of international employees (PCNs, TCNs, and HCNs) to compensate. Due to the complexity and expense of compensating PCNs, most of the discussion in this chapter addresses PCN compensation. Issues unique to compensating TCNs and HCNs are also described.

OBJECTIVES OF INTERNATIONAL COMPENSATION

When developing international compensation policies, a MNC seeks to satisfy several objectives. First, the policy should be consistent and fair in its treatment of all categories of international employees. The interests of the MNC are best served if all international employees are relatively satisfied with their compensation package and perceive that they are treated equitably. Second, the policy must work to attract and retain personnel in the areas where the MNC has the greatest needs and opportunities. Third, the policy should facilitate the transfer of international employees in the most cost-effective manner for the MNC. Fourth, the policy should be consistent with the overall strategy and structure of the MNC. Finally, compensation should serve to motivate employees. Some professional international HR managers would say that motivation is the major objective of their compensation programs.[3]

DESIGNING INTERNATIONAL COMPENSATION PACKAGES

In general, the first issue facing MNCs when designing international compensation policies is whether to establish an overall policy for all employees or to distinguish between PCNs and TCNs. This differentiation may diminish in the future, but it is currently very common for MNCs to distinguish between these two distinct groups. There is even a tendency for MNCs to differentiate among types of PCNs. Separate types of policies may be established based on the length of assignment (temporary transfer, permanent transfer, or continual relocation) or on the type of employee. Cash remuneration, special allowances, benefits, and pensions are determined in part by such classification. Short-term PCNs, for example, whose two- or three-year tours of duty abroad are interspersed with long periods at home, may be treated differently from career PCNs who spend most of their time working in various locations abroad. Both of these groups are different from TCNs, who often move from country to country in the employ of one MNC (or several) head-quartered in a country other than their own (for example, a Swiss banker, may be in charge of a West German branch of a British bank). In effect, these are the real global employees, the ones who can weave together the far-flung parts of a MNC. As the global MNC increases in importance, it is likely that the TCNs will become more valuable and thus be able to command levels of compensation equivalent to PCNs.

For PCNs, the most widely used policy emphasizes "keeping the expatriate whole" (that is, maintaining relativity to PCN colleagues plus compensating for the costs of international service).[4] The basis of this policy implies that foreign assignees should not suffer a material loss due to their transfer, and this is accomplished through the utilization of what is known as the balance-sheet approach. According to Reynolds,[5] "the balance-sheet approach to international compensation is a system designed to equalize the purchasing power of employees at comparable position levels living overseas and in the home country, and to provide incentives to offset qualitative differences between assignment locations." A typical balance sheet is shown in Figure 6–1. There are five major categories of outlays that cover all of the types of expenses incurred by expatriate families:

1. *Goods and services:* home-country outlays for items such as food, personal care, clothing, household furnishings, recreation, transportation, and medical care.

2. *Housing:* the major costs associated with the employees' principal residence.

3. *Income taxes:* payments to federal and local governments for personal income taxes.

4. *Reserve:* contributions to savings, payments for benefits, pension contributions, investments, education expenses, social security taxes, etc.

5. *Shipment and storage:* the major costs associated with shipping and storing personal and household effects.

Thus, MNCs seek to develop international packages that are competitive in all of the following aspects of compensation:

Salary
▸ home rate/home currency
▸ local rate/local currency
▸ salary adjustments or promotions—home or local standard

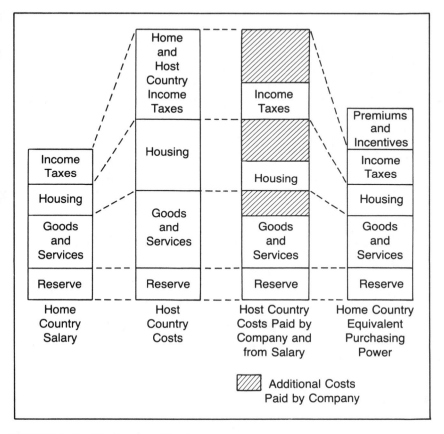

FIGURE 6-1 The Balance Sheet
SOURCE: C. Reynolds, "Compensation of Overseas Personnel," in *Handbook of Human Resource Administration* (2nd ed.), ed. J. J. Famularo (New York: McGraw-Hill, 1986), p. 51. Reprinted with permission.

▶ bonus — home or local currency, home or local standard
▶ stock options
▶ inducement payment/hardship premium — percent of salary or lump sum payment, home or local currency
▶ currency protection — discretion or split basis
▶ global salary and performance structures

Taxation
- ▶ tax protection
- ▶ tax equalization
- ▶ other services

Benefits
- ▶ home-country program
- ▶ local program
- ▶ social security program

Allowances
- ▶ cost-of-living allowances
- ▶ housing standard
- ▶ education
- ▶ relocation
- ▶ perquisites
- ▶ home leave
- ▶ shipping and storage

Although some of these aspects of international compensation may not apply to TCNs or HCNs, all do apply to PCNs. These aspects are now described in detail.

Base Salary

The term "base salary" acquires a somewhat different meaning when employees go abroad. At home, base salary denotes the amount of cash compensation that serves as a benchmark for other compensation elements (for example, bonuses and benefits). For PCNs, it is the primary component of a package of allowances, many of which are directly related to base salary (foreign service premium, cost-of-living allowances, housing allowances, and tax protection, for example) as well as the basis for in-service benefits and pension contributions. When applied to TCNs, base salary may mean the prevailing rate paid for a specific skill in the employee's home country. In the Schuler and Dowling survey,[6] all of the respondents indicated that their companies used local compensation levels as guidelines when developing HCN compensation policies. Conditions that force compensation policies to differ from those in the United States include: inflation/cost of living, housing, security, school costs, and taxation. For example, it is far less costly to recruit a construction engineer from Spain or Taiwan to work in the Middle East than from the United Kingdom or the United States. Consequently:

> More than half of American companies now tie base salaries to the home countries of the third-country national they employ, rather than to U.S. or host country salary structures, according to a survey of 117 international companies by Organization Resources Counsellors Inc. The number of companies doing this has risen frm 38% to more than 52% in just two years, and the trend includes those with small as well as large PCN populations. The primary objective is cost savings, since base pay levels of most other countries are currently below those of the U.S.[7]

The base salary of a PCN is usually paid either in the home currency at the home rate or in the local currency at a rate equivalent to the rate paid locally for the same job. Similarly, salary adjustments and promotional practices may be fashioned according to either home-country or local standards. In some select cases, global salary and performance structures have been implemented.

If the MNC utilizes any type of incentive bonus system, a policy is usually established. Bonuses may be according to either home- or host-country policies. Actual payments can be made in either local or foreign currency and may often be a combination of the two or at the choice of the recipient. For example, the majority of U.S. financial services companies have an overall policy of paying PCNs according to the U.S. salary structure (this includes bonus programs and salary increase practices). Most often, this compensation is paid partly in U.S. dollars and partly in the local currency. While the local currency portion is generally pegged to pay ordinary living expenses, bonuses are typically paid in U.S. dollars. Salary practices for TCNs tend to vary more widely and may be paid according to the home structure, a U.S. structure, or the host-country structure.

Questions that MNCs generally have to address when planning for their incentive bonuses include:

▸ What techniques can be used to provide management incentives abroad?

▸ Incentive bonuses help many companies achieve their objectives at home, but can they be used as effectively in subsidiary operations?

▸ How can companies design appropriate incentive bonuses for managers in an area suffering from intractable inflation?[8]

American MNCs frequently link stock opportunities to executive performance. Recent tax law changes in a number of western countries make stock ownership more feasible than in the past.[9]

Parent-country nationals often receive a salary premium as an inducement to accept a foreign assignment or to compensate for any hardship suffered due to the transfer. Under such circumstances, the definition of hardship, eligibility for the premium, and amount and timing of payment must be addressed. In cases in which hardship is determined, MNCs often refer to the U.S. Department of State's Hardship Post Differentials Guidelines to determine an appropriate level of payment. As Ruff and Jackson[10] have noted, however, there are many problems involved with international comparisons of the cost of living. It is important to note that TCNs do not receive these payments as often as PCNs. Foreign service inducements, if used, are most commonly made in the form of a percentage of salary, usually 5 to 40 percent of base pay. Such payments vary depending upon the assignment, actual hardship, tax consequences, and length of assignment. In addition, differentials may be considered; for example, a host country's work week may be longer than that of the home country, and a differential payment may be made in lieu of overtime, which is not normally paid to PCNs or TCNs.

Currency protection is also an issue affecting compensation. Several alternatives for this protection exist. Employees may have discretion over the currency used in payments, or a standard split basis for all PCNs may exist. A split basis may be applied on a case-by-case basis, depending upon the particular country assignment. With regard to local currency payments, a policy concerning exchange rate adjustments is necessary to assure that all employees are being treated fairly.

Taxation

Addressing tax protection and/or tax equalization can be extremely expensive as well as challenging for MNCs. According to the Schuler and Dowling survey:[11]

> For PCNs (and TCNs) in high tax countries the greatest challenge is tax effective compensation and reduction/avoidance of the pyramid effect of tax equalization. A senior executive earning of $100,000 in Belgium, for example, could cost a company close to $1.0 million in taxes over a 5–7 year period.

For the U.S. expatriate, an assignment abroad can mean being double-taxed — in the country of assignment and in the United States. This tax cost (although somewhat higher than most examples), combined with all of the other PCN costs, makes U.S. MNCs think twice about making use of expatriates. In fact, many U.S. MNCs could not afford to use expatriates if it were not for section 911 of the IRS code, which contains the foreign earned income exclusion provisions permitting a $70,000 deduction.

Under most tax equalization programs, companies withhold an amount equal to the home-country tax obligation of the PCN and then pay all taxes in the host country. An alternative approach is that of tax protection, in which the employee pays up to the amount of taxes equal to those he or she would pay based upon compensation in the home country. In such a situation, the employee is entitled to any windfall received if total taxes are less in the foreign country than in the home country. Other tax considerations in forming company policies involve state and local tax payments, tax return preparation, and the definition of an employee's total income on which the company is basing its calculations (for example, does total income include stock options or spouse's income?).

Tax equalization is by far the more common taxation policy used by MNCs. Thus, for a U.S. expatriate, tax payments equal to the liability of a U.S. taxpayer with the same income and family status are imposed on the employee's salary and bonus. Any additional premiums or allowances are typically paid by the company, tax-free to the employee. This seemingly straightforward policy actually illustrates the tremendous complexity in international compensation. In granting premiums or allowances, the MNC needs to determine the expatriate's tax status in the home country and in the host country and then decide which to pay. Because the decision can be costly to the individual, organizations can gain a competitive advantage in attracting employees through their compensation policies. This competitive advantage depends upon the definition of income covered by equalization, the type of hypothetical taxes to which the policy is applied, and the level of tax deductions allowed. Most MNCs consider both state and federal taxes of both the home country and the host country when designing their policies, but not all of them include spouse income under the policy.

As MNCs operate in more and more countries, they are subject to widely discrepant tax rates. A sample of this diversity is illustrated in Exhibit 6–1. Many MNCs have responded to this complexity and di-

EXHIBIT 6–1   Maximum Marginal Federal Tax Rates*

Country	1985 Maximum marginal rate	1988 Maximum marginal rate	Income level at which reached In local currency	In U.S. dollars**
Argentina	45%	38.25%	A416,500	$119,000
Australia	49	49	A$35,001	25,984
Belgium	72	70.8	BFr4,202,000	121,235
Brazil	60	50	Cz$2,784,600	38,536
Canada	34	29.87	Can$55,000	44,571
France	65	56.8	FFr720,000	128,251
Germany	56	56	DM260,000	157,100
Hong Kong	17.5	16.5	HK$300,000	38,462
Italy	65	62	Lit600,000,000	488,599
Japan	70	60	¥50,000,000	403,714
Korea	55	55	W60,000,000	79,915
Mexico	55	50	Ps45,063,804	20,484
Netherlands	72	72	Fi229,625	123,521
Singapore	40	33	S$400,000	200,100
Spain	66	56	Pta8,000,000	72,483
Sweden	50	45	SKr190,000	32,418
Switzerland	13.75	11.5	SFr423,600	310,557
United Kingdom	60	40	£19,300	36,415
United States	50	33	US$71,900	71,900
Venezuela	45	45	Bs8,000,000	271,647

*Maximum marginal rates are those applicable to resident citizens as of January 1, 1988, with one exception: the rate for the U.K. reflects April 1988 changes. Where different rates apply to married and single employees, the married employee rate is shown. Social security taxes are excluded.
**Based on April 1, 1988 exchange rates, adjusted for high inflation countries.
SOURCE: TPF&C

versity across countries by retaining the services of an international accounting firm to provide advice. Many MNCs also use internal and external accountants to prepare host-country and home-country tax returns for U.S. expatriates.

Wage levels also vary greatly across nations. When MNCs plan compensation packages, they need to consider how specific practices can be modified in each country to provide the most tax-effective, appropriate rewards for PCNs, HCNs, and TCNs within the framework of overall company policy.

The policies discussed in this section usually pertain to PCNs. In the case of TCNs, many different approaches have been used. Although a detailed analysis of each different approach is beyond the scope of this chapter, the major approaches include a U.S. balance sheet, a non-U.S. home-country balance sheet, a host-country package, a host-country package including extras, a U.S. salary including local benefits, or a U.S. package less tax equalization.[12]

Benefits

One international HRM manager has noted that the difficulties in international compensation "are not compensation so much as benefits. Pension plans are very difficult to deal with country to country as cultural practices vary endlessly. Transportability of plans, e.g., pension, medical, social security are very difficult to normalize."[13] MNCs need to address many issues when considering benefits, including:

▸ Whether or not to maintain expatriates in home-country programs, particularly if the company does not receive a tax deduction for it.

▸ Whether companies have the option of enrolling expatriates in host-country benefit programs and/or making up any difference in coverage.

▸ Whether host-country legislation regarding termination affects benefit entitlements.

▸ Whether expatriates should receive home-country or host-country social security benefits.

▸ Whether benefits should be maintained on a home-country or host-country basis, who is responsible for the cost, whether other benefits should be used to offset any shortfall in coverage, and whether home-country benefit programs should be exported to local nationals in foreign countries.

Most U.S. PCNs typically remain under their home-company's benefit program. For example, U.S. financial companies typically include PCNs in U.S. retirement/capital accumulation programs, medical/death/disability programs, and social security programs. With regard to social security, a recent Towers, Perrin, Forster & Crosby (TPF&C) survey[14] found:

Totalization agreements between the U.S. and Belgium, Canada, Italy, Norway, Switzerland, the U.K. and West Germany effectively eliminate dual social security coverage of citizens of one country working temporarily in another. Each agreement defines which country's coverage applies under specific employment situations. However, U.S. citizens can elect to be covered only by U.S. social security if they work for foreign subsidiaries of U.S. companies.

In some countries, PCNs cannot opt out of local social security programs. In such circumstances the MNC normally pays for these additional costs. European PCNs and TCNs enjoy portable social security benefits within the European Community. Laws governing private benefit practices differ from country to country, and company practices also vary. Multinationals have generally done a good job of planning for the private retirement needs of their PCN employees, but this is less the case for TCNs.[15] There are many reasons for this: TCNs may have little or no home-country social security coverage, they may have spent many years in countries that do not permit currency transfers of accrued benefit payments, or they may spend their final year or two of employment in a country where final average salary is in a currency that relates unfavorably to their home-country currency. How their benefits are calculated and what type of retirement plan applies to them may make the difference between a comfortable retirement in a country of their choice and a forced penurious retirement elsewhere.

As Figure 6–2 shows, parent-company plans rarely cover TCNs. American MNCs generally provide either host-country or umbrella plans, Japanese firms prefer host-country plans, and European MNCs often rely on home-country plans. Many companies believe that an umbrella plan is most compatible with their benefit philosophy. Such a plan may include a formal contract stipulating certain pension guarantees based on the final three years' average earnings of the TCN, offset by certain social security and statutory benefit entitlements and any local private plan benefits to which an employee may be entitled. When such plans are used, it is important to find a formula for calculating the benefits in more than one currency if the TCN moves to another country during the final period, as many do. Similarly, allowance must be made for currency conversions, indexation, if required, and many other factors, not least of which is determining what percentage of final average salary represents an equitable retirement benefit for a once-invaluable employee.

In addition to the above benefits, MNCs also provide vacations and

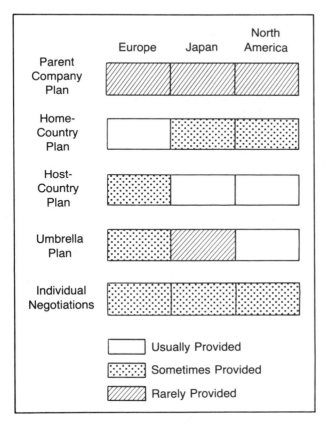

FIGURE 6-2 *Sources of TCN Retirement Income (by location of corporate headquarters)*
SOURCE: TPF&C

special leave. Included as part of the employee's regular vacation, annual home leave usually provides air fares for families to return to their home countries. Rest and rehabilitation leave, based on the conditions of the host country, also provides the employee's family with free air fares to a more comfortable location near the host country. In addition to rest and rehabilitation leave, emergency provisions are available in case of a death or illness in the family. Employees in hardship locations often receive additional leave expense payments and rest and rehabilitation periods.

Because of the complexities, challenges, and costs of providing benefits to international employees, MNCs need to address several questions when planning to do business abroad.

▸ With millions of dollars invested in benefit plans abroad, and with the costs of these plans steadily increasing, how can the MNC measure, control, and contain costs while keeping benefit promises to employees?

▸ Should benefit promises be reevaluated?

▸ Can benefits be reduced?

▸ Can better funding vehicles be found for pension investments?

▸ Can MNCs ensure that a proper charge to income is made for benefit plans abroad?

Allowances

Issues concerning allowances can be very challenging when establishing an overall compensation policy, partly because of the many types and forms that can exist. The *cost-of-living allowance*, which typically receives the most attention, involves a payment to compensate for differences in expenditures between the home and foreign country (for example, to account for inflation differentials). Often this allowance is difficult to determine and may include payments for housing and utilities, personal income tax, or discretionary items.[16]

The provision of a *housing allowance* implies that employees should be entitled to maintain their home-country living standards (or in some cases receive accommodation that is equivalent to that provided for similar foreign employees and peers). Such allowances are often paid on either an assessed or an actual basis. Other housing alternatives include company-provided housing, with or without employee obligation; a fixed housing allowance; or assessment of a portion of income, out of which actual housing costs are paid. Housing issues are often addressed on a case-by-case basis, but as globalization grows, formal policies become more necessary and efficient. Financial assistance and/or protection in connection with the sale or leasing of an expatriate's former residence is offered by almost all MNCs, although those in the finance industry tend to be the most generous, offering assistance in sale or leasing, payment of closing costs, payment of leasing management fees, rent protection, and equity protection. Third-country nationals receive these benefits much less frequently.

Education allowances for expatriates' children are also an integral part of any international compensation policy. Allowances for education can cover items such as tuition, language tuition, enrollment fees, books and supplies, transportation, room and board, and uniforms (outside of the U.S., it is quite common for high school students to wear uniforms). The level of education provided for, the adequacy of local schools, and transportation of dependents who are being educated in other locations may present problems for MNCs. Parent-country nationals and TCNs usually receive the same treatment concerning educational expenses. The cost of local or boarding school for dependent children is typically covered by the employer, although there may be restrictions according to availability of quality local schools and fees. Attendance at post-secondary schools may also be provided for when deemed necessary.

In the past, Japanese firms rarely sent an executive's family abroad, even when the assignment lasted several years, but this practice is changing. Now, when an executive's family accompanies him abroad, an allowance is customarily made of approximately 30 percent of base salary for his spouse and 5 percent for each child. When the family remains in Japan, an allowance equal to about 80 percent of the executive's base salary is paid.[17]

Relocation allowances usually cover moving, shipping, and storage charges; temporary living expenses; subsidies regarding appliance or car purchases (or sales); and down payments or lease-related charges. Allowances regarding perquisites (cars, club memberships, servants, and so on) may also need to be considered (usually for higher management positions). These allowances are often contingent upon tax equalization policies and practices in both the home and the host countries.

Multinationals generally pay allowances in order to encourage employees to take international assignments and to keep employees "whole" relative to home standards. In terms of housing, MNCs usually pay a tax-equalized housing allowance in order to discourage the purchase of housing and/or to compensate for higher housing costs. This allowance is adjusted periodically based on estimates of both local and foreign housing costs. For example, MNCs in the finance industry are beginning to purchase or lease company housing, which is provided directly through a lease or rent-back arrangement. Third-country nationals most often receive housing aid in the form of a fixed subsidy or a subsidized loan program. Similarly, almost all financial services companies compensate for differences in the cost of living between the PCNs' home and host countries. This payment is usually assessed by an independent organization and is in the form of cash. Very infrequently, a negative adjustment is made when the cost of living is lower in the foreign location. Normally, TCNs do not receive any type of cost-of-living allowance. Most financial companies pay a lump-sum relocation allowance (typically equivalent to one month's base salary) for expenses associated with moving. For both PCNs and TCNs, most organizations pay shipping and storage costs as well as transportation to and from the foreign location according to typical business travel standards. Cars are usually not shipped abroad, although some companies will provide sale protection.

For example, MNCs in the automobile industry pay cost-of-living allowances according to the host country's inflation index and exchange rate fluctuation. Housing and schooling allowances are also provided. Both Ford and General Motors either fully cover or substantially underwrite the costs of both housing and offspring education. Policies with regard to home-country housing, however, differ between the two companies. General Motors tries to encourage employees to retain ownership of their home-country housing. The company will pay all rental management fees and will reimburse the employee for up to six months' rent if the house remains unoccupied. If the employee decides to sell his or her home, the company will reimburse the selling costs. Ford provides its employees with three options: a program similar to GM's, with certain maximums on fees to be covered, a guaranteed house purchase offer, and a lease termination procedure. Both companies cover most moving and storage costs incurred by the employee.[18]

STRATEGIC IMPERATIVES

To succeed in an ever-changing international environment, MNCs must look beyond next year's goals and develop clear but flexible long-term compensation strategies. As Pucik[19] has noted:

> An effective managerial reward system should be linked to long-term corporate strategy and should anticipate changes in employees' valence of different organizational rewards. On the one hand, multinational settings make the complex task of developing such a system even more difficult; on the other hand, the fact that the corporation operates in many different environments permits the establishment of

unique reward programs, unavailable in more conventional environments.

In addition, MNCs need to match their compensation policies with their staffing policies and general HRM philosophies. If, for example, a MNC has an ethnocentric staffing policy, its compensation policy should be one of keeping the PCN whole. If, however, the staffing policy follows a geocentric approach (that is, staffing a position with the "best person," regardless of nationality) there may be no clear "home" for the TCN, and the MNC will need to consider establishing a system of international base pay for key managers paid in a major reserve currency such as the U.S. dollar or the Deutschmark. This system allows MNCs to deal with considerable variations in base salaries for managers, such as that noted in the following recent report.[20]

> In Switzerland, a department head working for a medium-sized company earns $60,000. The same executive in Germany earns only $49,000. But in the U.S., the equivalent job pays only $45,000, according to a survey by Business International Corporation. However, the gap increases as U.S. executives climb the corporate ladder. At the highest levels, CEOs in the U.S. average $727,000, while those in Switzerland average only $214,000 and in Germany only $171,000.

Further evidence of the disparity between management compensation across countries is shown in Figure 6–3, which compares total cash compensation for CEOs in twenty countries.

Termination Liabilities

MNCs need to consider the strategic consequences of a decision to terminate overseas operations. Most countries have some traditional or legally required practices that come into play in the event of a plant shutdown or substantial reduction in workforce.[21] In general, these practices create more extensive and costlier employer obligations than do the "marketplace" layoffs in the United States and Canada. One of the most costly obligations is the payment of cash indemnities, which are in addition to the individual termination payments that may be required by law, collective bargaining agreement, or individual contracts. These indemnities can range from as high as two years' pay in Mexico to a flat amount, adjusted for increases in the cost of living, in Belgium. In some

Argentina	36	/////////////
Australia	37	/////////////
Belgium	52	//////////////////
Brazil	42	///////////////
Canada	57	///////////////////
France	46	////////////////
Hong Kong	34	////////////
Italy	42	///////////////
Japan	50	//////////////////
Mexico	48	/////////////////
Netherlands	47	/////////////////
Singapore	48	/////////////////
Spain	38	//////////////
Sweden	37	/////////////
Switzerland	71	/////////////////////////
United Kingdom	38	//////////////
United States	100	/////////////////////////////////
Venezuela	52	//////////////////
West Germany	54	//////////////////

FIGURE 6-3 Average CEO Total Cash Compensation as a % of U.S. T.C.C. (in an operation with U.S. $100 million in annual sales)
Based on average 1984 exchange rates.
Saudi Arabia is omitted for lack of sufficient data.
SOURCE: TPF&C

countries, these costs are spelled out in collective agreements that may stipulate termination payments greater than those required by law. In other countries, the employer may have to negotiate the amounts with employees, unions, and often the government. An example of the estimated costs of these payments is shown in Figure 6-4.

In many countries, a company that wishes to close down or curtail operations also must develop a "Social Plan" or its equivalent, typically

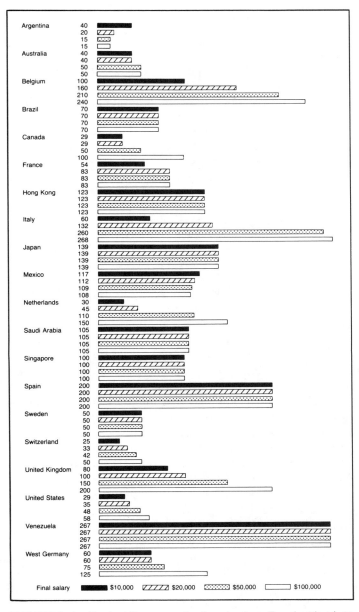

FIGURE 6-4 Typical Payments for Involuntary Termination* as a % of Annual Cash Remuneration in U.S. Dollars

*Payments include both severance pay and pay in lieu of notice. All employees are married, age 40, with children and 15 years of service.

SOURCE: TPF&C

133

in concert with unions and other interested parties. The "Plan" may cover continuation of pay, benefit plan coverage, retraining allowances, relocation expenses, and supplementation of statutory unemployment compensation. Frequently, a company planning a partial or total plant shutdown must present its case to a government agency. Authorities in The Netherlands, for example, may deny permission for a substantial reduction in workforce unless management is able to demonstrate that the cutback is absolutely necessary for economic reasons and that the company has an approved Social Plan.

Compensation Practices in Other Countries

Cash is, of course, the basis of compensation everywhere, but "pay" often includes additional noncash elements. In France, for example, subsidized transportation services and company restaurant lunches or luncheon vouchers are common. Workers in the Philippines receive a measure of rice, with better-quality rice provided to skilled and professional workers. In many countries, flour, grain, or potatoes are provided as pay supplements. Consumer product companies may offer their employees a choice of cash or the cash equivalent of their pay in company products at a discounted price. Employees are free to resell these products at a profit, thereby increasing their actual earnings. Voluntary noncash or "in kind" payments are made because they are tax effective. In some countries they may come to be regarded as acquired rights — payments to which employees are legally entitled.

In addition to pay practices that vary from country to country, MNCs must deal with salary management systems that differ radically from west to east. European and North American MNCs usually base compensation on the type of work individual employees or classes of employees perform and the skill required for each defined job position. In Hong Kong and Singapore, individual performance and skill can dramatically affect compensation. Japanese companies tend to pay employees according to their age and seniority as well as group or company performance, offering little or no pay differentials for individual performance or exceptional skills. Latin American firms often continue to pay aging, nonproductive workers as much as they do young, vigorous ones because they cannot force them to retire without making additional payments on top of termination indemnities. Clearly, a company cannot ignore the compensation practices of the countries in which it operates. Ignorance of local custom invites disaster; knowledge of the laws, practices, and employer obligations in each country should form the basis for all international compensation.

SUMMARY

A host of complexities arise when companies move from compensation at the domestic level to compensation in an international context. In addition to considering parent-country financial, legal, and customary practices, foreign standards and practices must also be taken into account. Many varying viewpoints — parent- and host-country companies, host governments, PCN/TCN employees and their families, and HCNs—must be considered in the development of a MNC's compensation agenda and goals.

In this chapter we have noted how these concerns may affect salary, taxation, benefits, and allowances as well as the issues that must be confronted in these areas. All of the components of international compensation should be combined and positioned within the long-term strategic goals of the MNC. Rather than being an auxiliary corporate concern, compensation programs should be used to further the international competitive standing of the MNC.

QUESTIONS

1. What should be the main objectives of international compensation policies?
2. Describe the issue of tax equalization and how MNCs deal with it.
3. Are there differences in salary compensation consideration for PCNs and TCNs? Cite reasons either for such differences or for the absence of differences.
4. What are the main points MNCs must consider when deciding how to provide benefits?
5. Why is it important for MNCs to understand the compensation practices of other countries?

FURTHER READING

1. M. Gajek and M. M. Sabo, "The Bottom Line: What HR Managers Need to Know About the New Expatriate Regulations," *Personnel Administrator*, 1986, pp. 87–92.

2. International Compensation Committee, National Foreign Trade Council. *Expatriate Compensation Manual.* New York: National Foreign Trade Council Inc., 1987.

3. J. M. Kadet and R. J. Gaughan, Jr., "Manage Expatriate Expenses for Capital Returns," *Personnel Journal*, 1987, pp. 66–76.

4. B. A. Murdock and B. Ramamurthy, "Containing Benefits Costs for Multinational Corporations," *Personnel Journal*, 1986, pp. 80–84.

5. M. O'Reilly, "Total Remuneration: The International View," *Compensation and Benefits Review*, 1988, pp. 68–71.

6. J. M. Putti and K. C. Wong, "Flexible Wage Systems in Newly Industrialized Countries," *Compensation and Benefits Review*, November–December 1988, pp. 46–55.

7. J. Rayman and B. Twinn, *Expatriate Compensation and Benefits: An Employer's Handbook.* London: Kogan Page, 1983.

8. B. J. Springer, "1992: The Impact on Compensation and Benefits in the European Community," *Compensation and Benefits Review*, July–August 1989, pp. 20–27.

9. R. J. Stone, "Pay and Perks for Overseas Executives," *Personnel Journal*, 1986, pp. 64–69.

NOTES

1. *Worldwide Total Remuneration* (New York: Towers, Perrin, Forster & Crosby, 1987).

2. R. S. Schuler and P. J. Dowling, "Survey of ASPA/I Members" (Stern School of Business, New York University, 1988).

3. C. Reynolds, "High Motivation and Low Cost Through Innovative International Compensation," *Proceedings* of ASPA's 40th National Conference (Boston, 1989).

4. See B. W. Teague, *Compensating Key Personnel Overseas* (New York: The Conference Board, 1972), for a discussion of the concept of keeping the expatriate "whole."

5. This discussion of the "balance sheet" approach is based on C. Reynolds, "Compensation of Overseas Personnel," in *Handbook of Human Resources Administration* (2nd ed.), ed. J. J. Famularo (New York: McGraw-Hill, 1986).

6. Schuler and Dowling, "Survey of ASPA/I Members."

7. *HR Reporter Update*, Vol. 3, No. 2 (February 1987) p. 2.

8. *Worldwide Total Remuneration.*

9. For a review of the issues involved in providing incentives for expatriate managers, see B. J. Brooks, "Long-term Incentives for the Foreign-Based Executive," *Compensation and Benefits Review*, Vol. 17, No. 3 (1985) pp. 46–53.

10. H. J. Ruff and G. I. Jackson, "Methodological Problems in International Comparisons of the Cost of Living," *Journal of International Business Studies*, Vol. 5, No. 2 (1974) pp. 57–67.

11. Schuler and Dowling, "Survey of ASPA/I Members."

12. For further information, see C. Reynolds, "Compensation of Overseas Personnel."

13. Schuler and Dowling, "Survey of ASPA/I Members."

14. *Worldwide Total Remuneration.*

15. Ibid.

16. See Ruff and Jackson, "Methodological Problems."

17. *Worldwide Total Remuneration.*

18. This information from MBA student projects done at the University of Michigan.

19. V. Pucik, "Strategic HRM in Multinational Corporations," in *Strategic Management of Multinational Corporations*, ed. H. V. Wortzel and L. H. Wortzel (New York: John Wiley, 1985) p. 430.

20. *HR Reporter Update*, Vol. 3, No. 1 (January 1987), p. 5.

21. Part of this section is adapted from R. L. Foltz and R. G. Foltz, "International Human Resource Management," in *Readings in Personnel and Human Resource Management* (3rd ed.), ed. R. S. Schuler, S. A. Youngblood, and V. L. Huber (St. Paul, Minn.: West Publishing Co., 1988).

CHAPTER 7

▼

International Labor Relations

▲

Before examining the key issues in international labor relations as they relate to MNCs, it is important to briefly discuss some introductory points concerning the field of international labor relations.[1] First, HR professionals must realize that many difficulties arise when comparing industrial (or labor) relations systems and behavior across national boundaries. For example, one labor relations concept may have different meanings in different industrial relations contexts.[2] Consider the concept of collective bargaining. In the United States it is understood to mean negotiations between the labor union local and management, but in Sweden and Germany the term refers to negotiations between an employers' organization and a trade union at the industry level. Cross-national differences also emerge when the objectives of the collective bargaining process and the enforceability of collective agreements are considered. To illustrate the former point, many European unions view collective bargaining as a form of class struggle, but in the United States the objective of collective bargaining is viewed mainly in economic terms.

Second, it is generally recognized in the international labor relations field that no industrial relations system can be understood without an appreciation of its historical origin.[3] As Schregle[4] has observed:

A comparative study of industrial relations shows that industrial relations phenomena are a very faithful expression of the society in which they operate, of its characteristic features and of the power relationships between different interest groups. Industrial relations cannot be understood without an understanding of the way in which rules are established and implemented and decisions are made in the society concerned.

Poole[5] has identified several factors that may underlie historical differences among trade unions:

▸ the mode of technology and industrial organization at critical stages of union development
▸ methods of union regulation by government
▸ ideological divisions within the trade union movement
▸ the influence of religious organizations on trade union development
▸ managerial strategies for labor relations in large corporations

The results of historical differences can be found in the structures of trade unions in various countries. As Exhibit 7–1 shows, there is considerable diversity in union structure across nations. There are, for example, industrial unions, which represent all grades of employees in an industry; craft unions, which are based on skilled occupational groupings across industries; conglomerate unions, which represent members in more than one industry; and general unions, which are open to almost all employees in the country. This diversity has a major influence on the collective bargaining process in various countries. The less one knows about how a structure came to develop in a distinctive way, the less likely one is to understand it. As Prahalad and Doz[6] note, the lack of familiarity of MNC managers with local industrial and political conditions has sometimes needlessly worsened conflict that a local firm would have been likely to resolve.[7]

KEY ISSUES IN INTERNATIONAL LABOR RELATIONS

This chapter focuses on the labor relations strategies adopted by MNCs rather than on the more general topic of comparative labor relations.[8] The central question for labor relations in an international context is

EXHIBIT 7-1 Trade Union Structure in Leading Western Industrial Societies

Australia	general, craft, industrial, white-collar
Belgium	industrial, professional, religious, public sector
Canada	industrial, craft, conglomerate
Denmark	general, craft, white-collar
Finland	industrial, white-collar, professional and technical
Great Britain	general, craft, industrial, white-collar, public sector
Japan	enterprise
The Netherlands	religious, conglomerate, white-collar
Norway	industrial, craft
Sweden	industrial, craft, white-collar and professional
Switzerland	industrial, craft, religious, white-collar
United States	industrial, craft, conglomerate, white-collar
West Germany	industrial, white-collar

SOURCE: M. Poole, *Industrial Relations: Origins and Patterns of National Diversity* (London: Routledge & Kegan Paul, 1986), p. 79.

that of the orientation of MNCs to organized labor. Because national differences in economic, political, and legal systems produce markedly different labor relations systems across countries, multinational firms generally delegate the management of labor relations to their foreign subsidiaries. Such a policy of decentralization does not mean that corporate headquarters will not exercise some degree of central coordination over labor relations strategy. Generally, there will be some form of corporate involvement or overview of labor agreements made by foreign subsidiaries because these agreements may affect the international plans of the corporation and/or create precedents for negotiations in other countries. Robock and Simmonds[9] note that where transnational sourcing patterns have been developed (that is, a subsidiary in one country relies on another foreign subsidiary as a source of components or as a user of its output), labor relations throughout the system become one of the key success factors in operating a global production strategy.[10]

Researchers have noted differences between European and U.S. MNCs in terms of headquarters involvement in labor relations. For example, studies by Hamill[11] have reported that U.S. MNCs exercise greater centralized control over labor relations compared to subsidiaries of British companies. Bean[12] cites three factors that may explain the greater degree of centralized control over labor relations exercised by U.S. MNCs:

▸ A number of studies[13] have shown that compared to European MNCs, U.S. firms tend to concentrate authority at corporate headquarters, with greater emphasis on formal management controls and a close reporting system (particularly within the area of financial control) to ensure that planning targets are met.

▸ European MNCs have tended to deal with labor unions at industry level (frequently through employer associations) rather than at company level. The opposite is more typical for U.S. firms. In the United States, employer associations have not played a key role in the industrial relations system, and company-based labor relations policies are the norm.[14]

▸ A final factor is the extent of the home product market. If domestic sales are large relative to overseas operations (as is the case with many U.S. companies), it is more likely that overseas operations will be regarded by the parent company as an extension of domestic operations. This is not the case for many European MNCs, whose international operations represent the major part of their business. Bean cites as examples the two leading Swiss MNCs, whose domestic sales represent less than 4 percent of their output. Lack of a large home market is a strong incentive to adapt to host-country institutions and norms.

An additional important factor is that of management attitudes or ideology.[15] Knowledge of management attitudes to unions may provide a more complete explanation of MNC labor relations behavior than sole reliance on a rational economic model. This is of particular relevance to U.S. MNCs, as union avoidance appears to be deeply rooted in the value systems of American managers.[16] As Exhibit 7-2 shows, the U.S. also has one of the lowest union density rates (the percentage of wage and salary employees who are union members) in the western world. Hence, U.S. managers are less likely to have extensive experience with unions compared to managers in many other countries.

Although there are several problems inherent in data collection for cross-national comparison of union density rates, several theories have been suggested to explain the variations between countries. Such theories consider economic factors such as wages, prices, and unemployment levels; social factors such as public support for unions; and political factors. Strategies utilized by labor, management, and governments have been indicated to be particularly important.[17]

EXHIBIT 7-2 Aggregate Union Density Rates in 1985[a] (percentage of wage and salary employees who are trade union members)

Australia[b]	46
Austria	61
Canada[c]	38
Denmark	93
France	17
West Germany	38
Italy	41
Japan[c]	29
Netherlands	28
Norway	65
Sweden	83
Britain[d]	52
U.S.A.[e]	17

Note: The table is based on the latest available figures from a variety of sources. It should be kept in mind that there are many problems in comparing union density rates across countries, reflecting 1) whether professional and employee associations are included, 2) the precise employee population used to obtain density statistics, and 3) the sources used to collect statistics in each country. Data refer to 1985 unless indicated otherwise in notes.

[a]Source for all European countries: J. Visser, "Trade Unionism in Western Europe: Present Situation and Prospects," *Labour and Society*, Vol. 13, No. 2 (1988) pp. 125–182. Data refer to employed persons only. Visser notes that density rates in Austria, Denmark, Norway, and Britain are overstated because of retired and self-employed members and suggests that these rates be adjusted 5–7 points down.

[b]1986 data. Source: Australian Bureau of Statistics, *Trade Union Members*, Catalogue No. 6325.0, August 1986.

[c]1984 data. Source: G. J. Bamber and R. D. Lansbury, eds., *International and Comparative Industrial Relations* (Sydney, Australia: Allen and Unwin, 1987).

[d]1984 data. Source: J. Visser, "Trade Unionism in Western Europe."

[e]1987 data. Source: U.S. Department of Labor, Bureau of Labor Statistics, *Employment and Earnings*, Vol. 35, No. 1 (January 1988) p. 222. Data refer to members of a labor union or an employee association similar to a union and exclude work-

ers who report no union affiliation but whose jobs are covered by a union or an employee association contract. If the latter group were included, the union density rate would be 19.

LABOR RELATIONS PRACTICES OF MNCs

Much of the literature on the labor relations practices of MNCs tends to be at a macro or comparative level, and there is a scarcity of research that examines labor relations practices at the enterprise level. An exception is the work of Hamill.[18] In a series of studies, Hamill surveyed U.S.-owned and British-owned MNCs operating in Britain to compare their labor relations practices, their decision-making practices with regard to labor relations, and their labor relations performance. First, he surveyed eighty-four U.S.-owned and fifty British-owned MNCs operating in three British industries to compare their labor relations practices with regard to the following factors:

▸ union recognition
▸ employer association membership
▸ management organization for labor relations purposes
▸ the state of their negotiating arrangements
▸ the level and nature of collective agreements
▸ grievance procedures
▸ wage payment systems
▸ level of wages and employee fringe benefits

The results indicated a number of differences in labor relations practices between the U.S.- and British-owned MNCs in the sample. The U.S. MNCs were less likely to recognize trade unions, preferred not to join employer associations, had more highly developed and specialized personnel departments at plant level, and tended to pay higher wages and have more generous employee fringe benefits than British firms.

A second study focused on labor relations decision making in MNCs.[19] Hamill conducted a series of interviews, mostly with personnel directors in the British subsidiaries of thirty companies. His basic conclusion was that the labor relations function within the MNC is far from monolithic, that is, wholly decentralized or centralized. The extent of corporate involvement in each subsidiary's labor relations was influenced by the following factors:

▸ The degree of inter-subsidiary production integration. A high degree of integration was found to be the most important factor leading to the centralization of the labor relations function within the MNCs studied.

▸ Whether the subsidiary was U.S.-owned or European-owned. The former were found to be much more centralized in labor relations decision making than the latter. Hamill attributed this difference in management procedures to the more integrated nature of U.S. MNCs, the greater divergence between British and U.S. labor relations systems than between Europe and Britain, and the more ethnocentric managerial style of U.S. MNCs.

▸ Whether subsidiaries were well-established indigenous firms acquired by a MNC or greenfield sites set up by a MNC. The former tended to be given much more autonomy over labor relations than the latter.

▸ Whether subsidiaries were performing well or poorly. Poor performance tended to be accompanied by increased corporate involvement in labor relations. When poor performance was due to labor relations problems, the MNC tended to attempt to introduce parent-country labor relations practices aimed at reducing industrial unrest or increasing productivity.

▸ Whether the MNC was a significant source of operating or investment funds for the subsidiary. If this was the case, there was increased corporate involvement in labor relations.

The third study by Hamill[20] examined strike-proneness of MNC subsidiaries and indigenous firms in Britain across three industries. Strike-proneness was measured by three variables—strike frequency, strike size, and strike duration. There was no difference across the two groups of firms with regard to strike frequency, but MNC subsidiaries did experience larger and longer strikes than local firms. Hamill suggests that this difference indicates that foreign-owned firms may be under less financial pressure to settle a strike quickly than local firms, possibly because they can switch production out of the country.

Commenting on the overall results of his research, Hamill[21] concludes that "general statements cannot be applied to the organization of the labor relations function within MNCs. Rather, different MNCs adopt different labor relations strategies in relation to the environmental factors peculiar to each firm. In other words, it is the type of multinational under consideration which is important rather than multinationality itself."

STRATEGIC ASPECTS OF INTERNATIONAL LABOR RELATIONS

Labor unions may constrain the choices of MNCs in three ways: (1) by influencing wage levels to the extent that cost structures may become noncompetitive, (2) by limiting the ability of MNCs to vary employment levels at will (that is, at their own discretion), and (3) by hindering or preventing global integration of the operations of MNCs.[22] We shall briefly examine each of these potential constraints.

Influencing Wage Levels

Although the importance of labor costs relative to other costs is decreasing, labor costs still play an important part in determining cost competitiveness in most industries. The influence of unions on wage levels is therefore important, and MNCs that fail to successfully manage their wage levels will suffer labor cost disadvantages that may narrow the strategic options available to the MNC.

Limiting Employment Level Variation

For many MNCs operating in Western Europe, Japan, and Australia, the inability to vary employment levels at will may be a more serious problem than wage level constraints. Many countries now have legislation that limits considerably the ability of firms to carry out redundancy programs unless they can show that structural conditions make these employment losses unavoidable. Frequently, the process of showing the need for redundancy programs is long and drawn out. Redundancy legislation in many countries frequently specifies that firms must compensate redundant employees through specified formulas such as one week's pay for each year of service. In many countries payments for involuntary terminations are rather substantial, especially in comparison with the United States. (See Figure 6–4, page 133 for graphic illustration of this point.) Figure 7–1 illustrates some typical average earnings in manufacturing. Labor unions influence this process in two ways: first, by lobbying their own national governments to introduce redundancy legislation, and second, by encouraging regulation of MNCs by international organizations such as the Organization for Economic Cooperation and Development (OECD). (Later in this chapter we describe the Badger case, which resulted in Raytheon finally accepting re-

Argentina	26	(dotted bar)
	18	(hatched bar)
Australia	72	(dotted bar)
	72	(hatched bar)
Belgium	130	(dotted bar)
	70	(hatched bar)
Brazil	18	(dotted bar)
	9	(hatched bar)
Canada	90	(dotted bar)
	90	(hatched bar)
France	87	(dotted bar)
	56	(hatched bar)
Hong Kong	13	(dotted bar)
	12	(hatched bar)
Italy	79	(dotted bar)
	58	(hatched bar)
Japan	61	(dotted bar)
	50	(hatched bar)
Mexico	27	(dotted bar)
	13	(hatched bar)
Netherlands	126	(dotted bar)
	67	(hatched bar)
Singapore	14	(dotted bar)
	19	(hatched bar)
Spain	60	(dotted bar)
	37	(hatched bar)
Sweden	125	(dotted bar)
	72	(hatched bar)
Switzerland	117	(dotted bar)
	75	(hatched bar)
United Kingdom	61	(dotted bar)
	46	(hatched bar)
United States	100	(dotted bar)
	100	(hatched bar)
Venezuela	31	(dotted bar)
	13	(hatched bar)
West Germany	124	(dotted bar)
	75	(hatched bar)
	1979	(dotted bar)
	1984	(hatched bar)

FIGURE 7-1 *Average Hourly Earnings in Manufacturing as a % of U.S. Earnings*

Based on average yearly exchange rates.

Saudi Arabia is omitted for lack of sufficient data.

sponsibility for severance payments to employees made redundant by the closing down of its Belgian subsidiary.) MNC managers who do not take these restrictions into account in their strategic planning may find their options severely limited.

Hindering Global Integration

In recognition of the above factors, many MNCs make a conscious decision not to integrate and rationalize their operations to the most efficient degree, because to do so could cause industrial and political problems. Prahalad and Doz[23] cite General Motors as an example of this suboptimization of integration. They alleged that in the early 1980s GM made substantial investments in Germany (matching its new investments in Austria and Spain) at the demand of the German metalworkers' union (one of the largest industrial unions in the western world) in order to foster good labor relations in Germany. One observer of the world auto industry suggested that car manufacturers were suboptimizing their manufacturing networks, partly to placate trade unions and partly to provide redundancy in sources to prevent localized social strife from paralyzing their network. Such suboptimization led to unit manufacturing costs 15 percent higher in Europe, on average, than an economically optimal network would have achieved. Commenting on this example, Prahalad and Doz conclude:

> Union influence thus not only delays the rationalization and integration of MNCs' manufacturing networks and increases the cost of such adjustments (not so much in the visible severance payments and "golden handshake" provisions as through economic losses incurred in the meantime), but also, at least in such industries as automobiles, permanently reduces the efficiency of the integrated MNC network. Therefore, treating labor relations as incidental and relegating them to the specialists in the various countries is inappropriate. In the same way as government policies need to be integrated into strategic choices, so do labor relations.

THE RESPONSE OF LABOR UNIONS TO MNCs

Labor union leaders have long seen the growth of MNCs as a threat to the bargaining power of labor because of the considerable power and influence of large MNCs. Kennedy[24] has identified the following seven characteristics of MNCs as the basis of labor union concern about MNCs:

1. Formidable financial resources. This includes the ability to absorb losses in a particular foreign subsidiary that is in dispute with a national union and still show an overall profit on worldwide operations.

2. Alternative sources of supply. This may take the form of an explicit "dual sourcing" policy to reduce the vulnerability of the corporation to a strike by any national union.

3. The ability to move production facilities to other countries.

4. Superior knowledge and expertise in labor relations.

5. A remote locus of authority (the corporate head office management of a MNC).

6. Production facilities in many industries. As Vernon[25] has noted, most MNCs operate in many product lines.

7. The capacity to stage an "investment strike" in which the multinational refuses to invest any additional funds in a plant, thus ensuring that the plant will become obsolete and economically noncompetitive.

The response of labor unions has been threefold: to form International Trade Secretariats (ITSs), to lobby for restrictive national legislation, and to try to achieve regulation of MNCs by international organizations. The function of an ITS is to provide worldwide links for the national unions in a particular trade or industry (metals, transport, and chemicals, for example).[26] The long-term goal of each ITS is to achieve transnational bargaining with each of the MNCs in its industry. To achieve this goal, according to Willatt,[27] each ITS is following a similar program. The elements of this program are (1) research and information, (2) organization of a company conference, (3) establishment of a company council, (4) company-wide union-management discussions, and (5) coordinated bargaining.

To date, the ITSs have met with limited success. The reasons for this lack of success have been summarized by Northrup[28] as (1) the generally good wages and working conditions paid by MNCs, (2) strong resistance from multinational managements, (3) conflicts within the labor movement, and (4) differing laws and customs in the labor relations area. In addition to the above, unions have conflicting national economic interests when dealing with MNCs. In times of economic downturn, these conflicts may become an insurmountable barrier for trade union officials. Blake[29] gives an example of such a situation. In the early 1970s the Ford Motor Company indicated that the labor climate in Britain was a disincentive to further investment in that country. In response, a group of Dutch businessmen urged Ford to consider The Netherlands for future investment. Despite strong criticism of Ford by British unions, the Dutch trade union leadership did not object to these suggestions that investment funds may be transferred to their country.

On a political level, the response of the labor unions has been to lobby for restrictive national legislation in the United States and Europe and the regulation of MNCs by international organizations. The motivation for labor unions to pursue restrictive national legislation is based on a desire to prevent the export of jobs through multinational investment policies. For example, in the United States, the AFL-CIO has lobbied strongly in this area.[30] To date, these attempts have been largely unsuccessful; with the increasing internationalization of business, it is difficult to see how governments will be persuaded to legislate in this area.

Attempts by labor unions to exert influence over MNCs with international organizations have met with some success. Through trade union federations such as the European Trade Union Confederation (ETUC) and the International Confederation of Free Trade Unions (ICFTU), the labor movement has been able to lobby the International Labor Organization (ILO), the United Nations Commission on Transnational Corporations (UNCTC), the Organization for Economic Cooperation and Development (OECD), and the European Community (EC). In 1977 the ILO adopted a code for MNCs (Tripartite Declaration of Principles Concerning MNCs and Social Policy), but the UNCTC has to date been concerned with more technical aspects of international business.[31]

The ILO code of conduct originally proposed in 1975 was influential in the drafting of the OECD Guidelines for MNCs that were approved in 1976. These voluntary guidelines cover disclosure of information, competition, financing, taxation, employment and industrial relations, and science and technology.[32] A key section of these guidelines is the *umbrella* or *chapeau clause* (the latter is the more common term in the literature) that precedes the guidelines. This clause states that MNCs should adhere to the guidelines "within the framework of law, regulations and prevailing labor relations and employment practices, in each of the countries in which they operate." Campbell and Rowan[33] state that employers have understood the chapeau clause to mean compliance with local law while labor unions have interpreted the clause to mean that the guidelines are a "supplement" to national law. The implication of this latter interpretation is significant: A company could be in violation of the OECD guidelines even though its activities have complied with national law and practice. Given the ambiguity of the chapeau clause and the fact that the OECD guidelines are voluntary, it is likely that this issue will remain controversial.

There is also some controversy in the literature regarding the effectiveness of the OECD guidelines in regulating multinational behavior.[34] This lack of agreement centers on assessments of the various challenges to the guidelines. The best known of these challenges is the Badger Case. In 1976 the Badger Company, a subsidiary of Raytheon, a U.S. MNC, decided to close its Belgian subsidiary, and a dispute arose concerning termination payments.[35] Badger (Belgium) NV had filed for bankruptcy, so the Belgian labor unions argued that Raytheon should assume the subsidiary's financial obligation. Raytheon refused, and the case was brought before the OECD by the Belgian government and the International Federation of Commercial, Clerical, Professional and Technical Employees (FIET), an international trade secretariat. The Committee on International Investments and MNCs (CIIME) of the OECD indicated that Paragraph 6 of the guidelines (concerned with plant closures) implied a "shared responsibility" by the subsidiary and the parent in the event of a plant closing. Following this clarification by the CIIME and a scaling down of initial demands, Badger executives and Belgian government officials negotiated a settlement of the case.

Blanpain[36] concluded that the Badger case made clear the responsibility of the parent company for the financial liability of its subsidiary, but that this responsibility was not unqualified. As to whether the Badger case proved the "effectiveness" of the OECD guidelines, Jain[37] and Campbell and Rowan[38] point out that the Belgian unions devoted considerable resources to make this a test case. In addition, they had assistance from both American unions (who through the AFL-CIO lobbied the U.S. State Department) and the Belgian government in their negotiations with the OECD and Badger executives. Liebhaberg[39] is more specific in his assessment:

> Despite an outcome which those in favor of supervision consider to be positive, the Badger Case is a clear demonstration of one of the weaknesses in the OECD's instrument, namely that it does not represent any sort of formal undertaking on the part of the twenty-four member states which are signatories to it. The social forces of each separate country must apply pressure on their respective governments if they want the guidelines applied.

Recognizing the limitations of voluntary codes of conduct, European labor unions have also lobbied the Commission of the European

Community (EC) to regulate the activities of MNCs. As Latta and Bellace[40] point out, unlike the OECD, the Commission of the EC can translate guidelines into law, and through its company law and social affairs directorates has developed a number of proposals concerning disclosure of information to make MNCs more "transparent." Exhibit 7–3 summarizes the various directives from the EC concerning information disclosure. The most contentious directive is the "Vredeling" directive associated with Henk Vredeling, a former Dutch member of the EC Commission.[41] The Vredeling directive would require a multinational company to disclose data on specified items at specified intervals (regardless of whether a request has been made for this information or not) and to consult with employees on certain decisions before the proposed action. The directive also states that the parent company or "relevant decision-making center" must notify local subsidiaries of planned changes. Bellace and Latta[42] have summarized the implications of the Vredeling proposal as follows:

EXHIBIT 7–3 European Community Directives on Disclosure of Company Information to Unions

Company Law	
Fifth Directive	On employee participation on company boards
Seventh Directive	On group accounts for European subsidiaries
Ninth Directive	On the formation and operation of groups of companies
Social Affairs	
Collective Redundancies	On employee representatives' rights to information and consultation in the event of lay-offs or closure
Acquired Rights of Workers on Transfers of Undertakings	On the safeguarding of employees in the event of a change of ownership of all or part of a business
"Vredeling" directive	On the rights of employees in large, complex companies to information and consultation on certain issues

SOURCE: Adapted from G. W. Latta and J. R. Bellace, "Making the Corporation Transparent: Prelude to Multinational Bargaining," *Columbia Journal of World Business*, Vol. 18, No. 2 (1983) p. 76.

Companies would be required to give prospective data on the future plans of the corporation as a whole and not just historical data on specific subsidiaries. The intention is to build a picture of the overall strategic planning of the company as well as providing more limited operational data. . . . By providing unions with information which gives a much clearer picture of the MNC's long-term plans, the Vredeling directive would establish the base for coordinating union activity against one MNC.

Not surprisingly, the Vredeling proposal has met with considerable opposition both from employer's representatives and the Thatcher government in Britain.[43] The British have argued that employee involvement in consultation and decision making should be voluntary and are critical of the cumbersome nature of EC legislation in this area. This opposition has led to considerable delay, and the Council of Ministers (which exercises the legislative power of the EC) has yet to approve the revised Vredeling directive it received from the European Commission in June 1983. With the advent of the unified European market in 1992, however, there has been further discussion within the EC of the need to develop a "European industrial relations area," and the EC Council of Ministers has agreed to resume discussion of the Vredeling directive. As Northrup, Campbell, and Slowinski[44] note:

The value of informing and consulting employees and their representatives, and, indeed, of building consensus between labor and management on the several challenges facing European industry, is questioned by no one. A resurgence of international labor-management consultation attests to this. The question remains whether these processes can or should be legislated.

SUMMARY

The literature we have reviewed in this chapter indicates that there are several types of collective bargaining arrangements used by unions in dealing with MNCs. Transnational collective bargaining, however, has yet to be attained by unions. As Enderwick[45] has stated:

The international operations of MNCs do create considerable impediments in effectively segmenting labor groups by national boundaries and stratifying groups within and between nations. Combining recognition of the overt segmentation effects of international business with an understanding of the dynamics of direct investment yields the conclusion that general multinational collective bargaining is likely to remain a remote possibility.

Enderwick argues that labor unions should opt for less ambitious strategies in dealing with MNCs such as (1) strengthening national union involvement in plant-based and company-based bargaining, (2) supporting research on the vulnerability of selective MNCs, and (3) consolidating the activities of company-based ITSs. It is likely that labor unions will pursue the above strategies plus lobby for regulation of MNCs through the EC and United Nations.

As we discussed in the chapter, the area of international labor relations is extremely complex. Further research is needed on how MNCs view the ongoing developments in the field and whether these developments will influence the overall business strategy of the enterprise. More also needs to be known on how MNCs implement labor relations policy in various countries. Recent work by Hamill[46] on the labor relations policy of a number of MNCs operating in Britain provides an excellent example of research that is helping us to obtain this much needed information. More specific research suggestions for this and all other activities in international HRM are offered in the Appendix.

QUESTIONS

1. Why is it important to understand the historical origins of national industrial relations systems?
2. In what ways can labor unions constrain the strategic choices of MNCs?
3. Identify four characteristics of MNCs that give labor unions cause for concern.
4. How have labor unions responded to MNCs? Have these responses been successful?
5. What is the Vredeling directive, and why is it important for European labor relations?

FURTHER READING

1. G. B. J. Bomers and R. B. Peterson, "Multinational Corporations and Industrial Relations: The Case of West Germany and the Netherlands," *British Journal of Industrial Relations*, March 1977, pp. 45–62.

2. *Columbia Journal of World Business*, Vol. 18, No. 2 (1983). Focus issue on international labor.

3. R. J. Flanagan and A. R. Weber, eds., *Bargaining Without Boundaries*. Chicago: University of Chicago Press, 1974.

4. "The Looming Labour Crunch," *International Management*, Vol. 44, No. 2 (1989) pp. 26–31.

5. M. Poole, "Managerial Strategies and 'Styles' in Industrial Relations: A Comparative Analysis," *Journal of General Management*, Vol. 12, No. 1 (1986) pp. 40–53.

6. R. S. Schuler, "Strategic Human Resource Management and Industrial Relations," *Human Relations*, Vol. 42, No. 2 (1989) pp. 157–184.

7. *Trade Unions of the World, 1989–1990*. 2nd ed. (Essex, England: Longman, 1989.)

NOTES

1. These introductory comments are drawn from the following article: J. Schregle, "Comparative Industrial Relations: Pitfalls and Potential," *International Labour Review*, Vol. 120, No. 1 (1981) pp. 15–30.

2. This point is also referred to as the "emic-etic" problem. See the Appendix of this text (Research Issues in International HRM) for a detailed discussion of this point.

3. O. Kahn-Freund, *Labor Relations: Heritage and Adjustment* (Oxford: Oxford University Press, 1979).

4. Schregle, "Comparative Industrial Relations," p. 28.

5. M. Poole, *Industrial Relations: Origins and Patterns of National Diversity* (London: Routledge, 1986).

6. C. K. Prahalad and Y. L. Doz, *The Multinational Mission: Balancing Local Demands and Global Vision* (New York: The Free Press, 1987).

7. We noted in Chapter 3 that many U.S. MNCs are reducing the number of expatriates on overseas assignment (see S. J. Kobrin, "Expatriate Reduction and Strategic Control in American Multinational Corporations," *Human Resource Management*, Vol. 27, No. 1 (1988) pp. 63–75.) With regard to labor relations, this has the effect of reducing the opportunities of U.S. managers to gain firsthand experience of labor relations in various countries.

8. See T. Kennedy, *European Labor Relations* (Lexington, Mass.: Lexington Books, 1980); R. Bean, *Comparative Industrial Relations: An Introduction to Cross-National Perspectives* (New York: St. Martin's Press, 1985); Poole,

Industrial Relations; and G. J. Bamber and R. D. Lansbury, eds., *International and Comparative Industrial Relations* (Sydney: Allen & Unwin, 1987) for general reviews of the comparative labor relations literature.

9. S. H. Robock and K. Simmonds, *International Business and Multinational Enterprises,* 4th ed. (Homewood, Ill.: Irwin, 1989).

10. See D. F. Hefler, "Global Sourcing: Offshore Investment Strategy for the 1980s," *Journal of Business Strategy,* Vol. 2, No. 1 (1981) pp. 7–12. Labor relations also become rather complex when MNCs operate in many different countries. Worldwide, there is a great diversity in industrial relations and unionization, in terms of both the context and legal requirements and the sophistication and suitability for application in an industrial/service-based economy. For more on diversity, see R. Blanpain, ed., *Comparative Labour Law and Industrial Relations in Industrialized Market Economies,* 4th ed. (Deventer, Netherlands: Kluwer, 1990).

11. J. Hamill, "The Labor Relations Practices of Foreign-Owned and Indigenous Firms," *Employee Relations,* Vol. 5, No. 1 (1983) pp. 14–16; J. Hamill, "Multinational Corporations and Industrial Relations in the U.K.," *Employee Relations,* Vol. 6, No. 5 (1984) pp. 12–16. See also B. C. Roberts and J. May, "The Response of Multinational Enterprises to International Trade Union Pressures," *British Journal of Industrial Relations,* Vol. 12 (1974) pp. 403–416.

12. Bean, *Comparative Industrial Relations.*

13. See J. La Palombara and S. Blank, *Multinational Corporations and National Elites: A Study of Tensions* (New York: The Conference Board, 1976); A. B. Sim, "Decentralized Management of Subsidiaries and Their Performance: A Comparative Study of American, British, and Japanese Subsidiaries in Malaysia," *Management International Review,* Vol. 17, No. 2 (1977) pp. 45–51; and Y. K. Shetty, "Managing the Multinational Corporation: European and American Styles," *Management International Review,* Vol. 19, No. 3 (1979) pp. 39–48.

14. See D. Bok, "Reflections on the Distinctive Character of American Labor Law," *Harvard Law Review,* Vol. 84 (1971) pp. 1394–1463; and J. P. Windmuller and A. Gladstone, eds., *Employers Associations and Industrial Relations: A Comparative Study* (Oxford: Clarendon Press, 1984).

15. For a lucid discussion of the importance of understanding ideology, see G. C. Lodge, "Ideological Implications of Changes in Human Resource Management," in *HRM Trends & Challenges,* ed. R. E. Walton and P. R. Lawrence (Boston: Harvard Business School Press, 1985).

16. T. A. Kochan, R. B. McKersie and P. Capelli, "Strategic Choice and Industrial Relations Theory," *Industrial Relations,* Vol. 23, No. 1 (1984) pp. 16–39.

17. See Bean, *Comparative Industrial Relations;* Poole, *Industrial Relations;* and J. Visser, "Trade Unionism in Western Europe: Present Situation and Prospects," *Labour and Society,* Vol. 13, No. 2 (1988) pp. 125–182.

18. Hamill, "Labor Relations Practices" and "Multinational Corporations and Industrial Relations"; and J. Hamill, "Labor Relations Decision Making Within Multinational Corporations," *Industrial Relations Journal,* Vol. 15, No. 2 (1984) pp. 30–34.

19. Hamill, "Labor Relations Decision Making."

20. Hamill, "Multinational Corporations and Industrial Relations."

21. Hamill, "Labor Relations Decision Making," p. 34.

22. This section is based in part on Chapter 5, "The Impact of Organized Labor," in Prahalad and Doz, *The Multinational Mission.*

23. Ibid.

24. Kennedy, *European Labor Relations.*

25. R. Vernon, *Storm Over the Multinationals: The Real Issues* (Cambridge, Mass.: Harvard University Press, 1977).

26. For a detailed analysis of ITSs, see R. Neuhaus, *International Trade Secretariats: Objectives, Organization, Activities,* 2nd ed. (Bonn, Federal Republic of Germany: Friedrich-Ebert-Stiftung, 1982).

27. N. Willatt, *Multinational Unions* (London: Financial Times, 1974).

28. H. R. Northrup, "Why Multinational Bargaining Neither Exists nor is Desirable," *Labor Law Journal,* Vol. 29, No. 6 (1978) pp. 330–342.

29. D. Blake, "Corporate Structure and International Unionism," *Columbia Journal of World Business,* Vol. 7, No. 2 (1972) pp. 19–26.

30. See Kennedy, *European Labor Relations;* and R. B. Helfgott, "American Unions and Multinational Enterprises: A Case of Misplaced Emphasis," *Columbia Journal of World Business,* Vol. 18, No. 2 (1983) pp. 81–86.

31. For example, see the following UNCTC reports: *Transborder Data Flows: Transnational Corporations and Remote-Sensing Data* (New York: United Nations, 1984); and *Transnational Corporations and International Trade: Selected Issues* (New York: United Nations, 1985).

32. For a detailed description and analysis of the OECD Guidelines for Multinational Enterprises, see D. C. Campbell and R. L. Rowan, *Multinational Enterprises and the OECD Industrial Relations Guidelines* (Philadelphia: Industrial Research Unit of The Wharton School, University of Pennsylvania, 1983); and R. Blanpain, *The OECD Guidelines for Multinational Enterprises and Labour Relations, 1982–1984: Experiences and Review* (Deventer, Netherlands: Kluwer, 1985).

33. Campbell and Rowan, *Multinational Enterprises and the OECD Industrial Relations Guidelines.*

34. J. Rojot, "The 1984 Revision of the OECD Guidelines for Multinational Enterprises," *British Journal of Industrial Relations*, Vol. 23, No. 3 (1985) pp. 379–397.

35. For a detailed account of this case see R. Blanpain, *The Badger Case and the OECD Guidelines for Multinational Enterprises* (Deventer, Netherlands: Kluwer, 1977).

36. R. Blanpain, *The OECD Guidelines for Multinational Enterprises and Labour Relations, 1976–1979: Experience and Review* (Deventer, Netherlands: Kluwer, 1979).

37. H. C. Jain, "Disinvestment and the Multinational Employer — A Case History from Belgium," *Personnel Journal*, Vol. 59, No. 3 (1980) pp. 201–205.

38. Campbell and Rowan, *Multinational Enterprises and the OECD Industrial Relations Guidelines*.

39. B. Liebhaberg, *Industrial Relations and Multinational Corporations in Europe* (London: Gower, 1980), p. 85.

40. G. W. Latta and J. R. Bellace, "Making the Corporation Transparent: Prelude to Multinational Bargaining," *Columbia Journal of World Business*, Vol. 18, No. 2 (1983) pp. 73–80.

41. For a detailed analysis of the Vredeling directive see D. Van Den Bulcke, "Decision Making in Multinational Enterprises and the Information and Consultation of Employees: The Proposed Vredeling Directive of the EC Commission," *International Studies of Management and Organization*, Vol. 14, No. 1 (1984) pp. 36–60.

42. Latta and Bellace, "Making the Corporation Transparent," p. 76.

43. P. Enderwick, *Multinational Business and Labor* (London: Croom Helm, 1985).

44. H. R. Northrup, D. C. Campbell, and B. J. Slowinski, "Multinational Union-Management Consultation in Europe: Resurgence in the 1980s?" *International Labour Review*, Vol. 127, No. 5 (1988) pp. 525–543.

45. P. Enderwick, "The Labor Utilization Practices of Multinationals and Obstacles to Multinational Collective Bargaining," *Journal of Industrial Relations*, Vol. 26, No. 3 (1984) pp. 345–364.

46. Hamill, "Labor Relations Practices"; "Multinational Corporations and Industrial Relations"; and "Labor Relations Decision Making."

CHAPTER 8

▼

Epilogue

▲

Our aim in this book has been to examine the international dimensions of HRM. It is clear that there is a need for more international HRM research and case study material. We concur with the conclusion by Laurent[1] that the field of international HRM is still in its infancy. It is important to note, however, that international HRM has only recently emerged as a field of inquiry within the HRM discipline, and progress to date in this field should be viewed from a historical perspective. Leap and Oliva[2] have noted that it is only during the past twenty years that HRM has developed as a distinct area of academic inquiry, and its evolution has been primarily shaped by the external stimuli of political, legal, social, and economic factors. The development of international business as an academic discipline is being shaped by similar external stimuli. As international business develops from its present academic base in economics, finance, and marketing, the importance of human resource issues in international operations will be gradually recognized, as they have been in the management of domestic business operations.[3]

There are some encouraging signs that international HRM is beginning to come of age. For example, the International Chapter of the Society for Human Resource Management (formerly ASPA/I) and the Human Resource Planning Society are gaining recognition as key sources of expertise in the field, and their annual conferences are an important source of information on current practices and trends. There is also increasing interest in the activities of the World Federation of Personnel Management Associations (WFPMA).[4] The WFPMA consists of thirty-nine national personnel management associations divided into four principal geographical groupings: the Society for Human Resource Management (SHRM), the European Association for Personnel Management (EAPM), the Inter-American Federation of Personnel Management (FIDAP), and the Asia Pacific Federation of Personnel Management Associations (APFPMA). The proposed integration of the European Community in 1992 will also bring increased attention to the field of international HRM as firms examine the implications of this potentially dramatic development in world business. As an example of this interest, the Institute of Personnel Management in Britain has recently conducted a study of the HR implications of an integrated market in Europe.[5]

We noted in Chapter 1 that the "attitudes of senior management to international operations" formed an important variable with respect to the development of international HR skills and capability in a firm. A recent survey of 1,500 senior executives in 20 countries conducted by the graduate school of business at Columbia University shows some interesting differences between U.S. and foreign executives with regard to the importance placed on developing an international outlook.[6] As Exhibit 8–1 shows, U.S. executives in this survey placed less emphasis on the importance of an international outlook, experience outside home country, and training in foreign languages than foreign executives when describing attributes that were "very important for the CEO of tomorrow."

EXHIBIT 8–1   Percent of U.S. and Foreign Executives Describing an Attribute as "Very Important for the CEO of Tomorrow"

Valued Management Practices	U.S.	Foreign
Emphasizes international outlook	62%	82%
Experienced outside home country	35%	70%
Trained in foreign language	19%	64%

SOURCE: *Fortune* © 1989 The Time Inc. Magazine Company. May 22, 1989, p. 112.

Thus, even though U.S. MNCs are investing heavily in Europe and other parts of the world,[7] there appears to be a lag between the investment behavior of corporations and the attitudes of the executives required to effectively manage international operations. Commenting on this survey, Lester Korn (chairman of Korn/Ferry International, a leading executive search firm) stated:[8]

> A "Copernican revolution" must take place in the attitudes of American CEOs as the international economy no longer revolves around the U.S., and the world market is shared by many strong players . . . . While U.S. executives have identified this change, they still place far less importance on having an international outlook than do the foreign executives surveyed.

It is inevitable that as more and more U.S. firms become involved in international business or are forced to compete against foreign firms in their domestic markets, the attitudes of the senior managers in these firms toward international issues will change. As we discussed in Chapter 2, the needs of global business in the 1990s will require a careful monitoring of conditions in the environment and planning of competitive strategies in advance. To operationalize international marketing or financial strategies, managers will need to consider appropriate human resource strategies. It is difficult to develop a comprehensive international human resource strategy to match a MNC corporate or business strategy if senior managers allow home-country attitudes to overly influence and limit the scope of the strategy formulation process. The challenge for HR managers is to both manage the complexity of HR operations in an international environment and influence the views of managers in other functional areas.

NOTES

1. A. Laurent, "The Cross-Cultural Puzzle of International Human Resource Management," *Human Resource Management*, Vol. 25 (1986) pp. 91–102.

2. T. Leap and T. Oliva, "General Systems Precursor Theory as a Supplement to Wren's Framework for Studying Management History: The Case of Human Resource/Personnel Management," *Human Relations*, Vol. 36 (1983) pp. 626–640.

3. For a more detailed discussion of this point, see P. J. Dowling, "Human Resource Issues in International Business," *Syracuse Journal of International Law and Commerce*, Vol. 13, No. 2 (1986) p. 269.

4. The WFPMA is a supporter of international research on personnel management. For example, they recently funded an excellent study: N. K. Napier and R. B. Peterson, *An International Perspective on Personnel Management* (Neutral Bay Junction, Australia, WFPMA, 1989). To assist HR professionals being exposed to international HR for the first time, the International Chapter of the Society for Human Resource Management conducts a "Primer" as part of its annual conference. The chapter has also published the "International Human Resource Reference Guide" for HR professionals looking for basic information.

5. *Personnel Management and the Single European Market* (London: Institute of Personnel Management, 1988).

6. This survey was reported in an article by L. B. Korn, "How the Next CEO Will be Different," *Fortune*, May 22, 1989, pp. 111–113.

7. For an example of current figures on U.S. investment in Europe, see "American Firms and Europe," *The Economist*, May 13, 1989, pp. 70–72.

8. Korn, "How the Next CEO Will be Different," p. 111.

Appendix: Research Issues in International HRM

In this text we have frequently commented that there is a scarcity of international research (in HRM and the field of management generally) to assist managers and HRM practitioners. There are a number of reasons for this lack of international research. First, the field of international management has in the past been regarded as a marginal academic area by many management researchers. As Schollhammer[1] has noted, much of the field of international management has been criticized as (1) descriptive and lacking in analytical rigor, (2) ad hoc and expedient in research design and planning, (3) self-centered in the sense that the existing research literature is frequently ignored, and (4) lacking a sustained research effort to develop case material.

A second reason for the lack of international research is cost. International studies are invariably more expensive than domestic studies, and this is a liability for international researchers in a competitive research funding environment.[2] In addition, international research takes more time, involves more travel, and frequently requires the cooperation of host-country organizations, government officials, and researchers. Development of a stream of research is consequently much more difficult.

Third, there are major methodological problems involved in the area of international management. These problems greatly increase the complexity of doing international research and, as Adler[3] has noted, frequently are impossible to solve with the rigor usually required of within-culture studies by journal editors and reviewers. The major methodological problems in this area are (1) defining culture, (2) the emic-etic distinction, (3) static group comparisons, and (4) translation and stimulus equivalence. We shall briefly examine each of these problems, as an appreciation of these issues informs our discussion of international HRM.

DEFINING CULTURE

Culture has been defined by Geertz[4] as "a system of inherited conceptions . . . by means of which men communicate, perpetuate, and develop their knowledge about attitudes towards life." Although there appears to be widespread acceptance at a general level of definitions such as Geertz's there is little agreement about either an exact definition of culture or the operationalization of this concept.[5]

For many researchers, culture has become an omnibus variable, representing a range of social, historic, economic, and political factors, invoked post hoc to explain similarity or dissimilarity in the results of a study. As Bhagat and McQuaid[6] have noted, "culture has often served simply as a synonym for nation without any further conceptual grounding. In effect, national differences found in the characteristics of organizations or their members have been interpreted as cultural differences." To reduce these difficulties, researchers must specify their definition of culture a priori rather than post hoc and be careful not to assume that national differences necessarily represent cultural differences.

THE EMIC-ETIC DISTINCTION

A second methodological issue in international research is the emic-etic distinction.[7] Emic refers to culture-specific aspects of concepts or behavior, and etic refers to culture-common aspects. These terms have been borrowed from linguistics: A phon*emic* system documents meaningful sounds specific to a given language, and a phon*etic* system organizes all sounds that have meaning in any language.[8]

Both the emic and etic approaches are legitimate research orientations. A major problem may arise, however, if a researcher imposes an etic approach (that is, assumes universality across cultures) when there is little or no evidence for doing so. A well-known example of an imposed etic approach is the convergence hypothesis that dominated much of U.S. and European management research in the 1950s and

1960s. This approach was based on two key assumptions.[9] The first assumption was that there were principles of sound management that held regardless of national environments. Thus, the existence of local or national practices that deviated from these principles simply indicated a need to change these local practices. The second assumption said that the universality of sound management practices would lead to societies becoming more and more alike in the future. Given that the United States was the leading industrial economy, the point of convergence would be toward the U.S. model.

Adoption of the convergence hypothesis has led to some rather poor predictions of future performance. For example, writing in the late 1950s, Harbison[10] concluded the following with regard to the Japanese managerial system: "Unless basic rather than trivial or technical changes in the broad philosophy of organization building are forthcoming, Japan is destined to fall behind in the ranks of modern industrialized nations."

To use Kuhn's[11] terminology, the convergence hypothesis became an established paradigm that many researchers found difficult to give up, despite a growing body of evidence supporting a divergence hypothesis. In an important paper reviewing the convergence/divergence debate, Child[12] made the point that there is evidence for both convergence and divergence. The majority of the convergence studies, however, focus on macrolevel variables (for example, structure and technology used by organizations across cultures), and the majority of the divergence studies focus on microlevel variables (for example, the behavior of people within organizations). His conclusion was that although organizations in different countries are becoming more alike (an etic or convergence approach), the behavior of individuals within these organizations is maintaining its cultural specificity (an emic or divergence approach). As noted above, both emic and etic approaches are legitimate research orientations, but methodological difficulties may arise if the distinction between these two approaches is ignored or if unwarranted universality assumptions are made.

STATIC GROUP COMPARISONS

A third methodological issue in international research is that virtually all cross-cultural comparisons are based on "static group designs."[13] The difficulty with static group comparisons in international research is that subjects are not randomly assigned from a superordinate population to different levels of a treatment variable. In practice, it is impossible for cross-cultural researchers to avoid this methodological problem. This difficulty is further compounded by ill-defined notions of culture as an independent variable. As Malpass[14] has observed, "No matter what attribute of culture the investigator prefers to focus upon or to interpret as the causative variable, any other variable correlated with the alleged causative variable could potentially serve in an alternative explanation of a mean difference between two or more local populations." As a practical solution to this problem, Malpass recommends that investigators should attempt to obtain data on as many rival explanations as possible and then demonstrate that they are less plausible (by conducting post hoc statistical analyses, for example) than the investigator's favored interpretation.[15]

TRANSLATION AND STIMULUS EQUIVALENCE

A fourth methodological issue in international research is that of translation and stimulus equivalence. Researchers need to be aware that problems may arise when translating concepts central to one culture into the language of another culture. Triandis and Brislin[16] note that the problem of translation has received a great deal of attention in the literature[17] and that translation problems should be "a starting point for research rather than a frustrating end to one's aspirations for data collection." Using methods such as the decentering technique,[18] which involves translating from the original to the target language and back again through several iterations, a researcher can test to see if there is any emic coloring of the concepts under investigation. If there are few differences between the original and target translation, then stimulus equivalence has been demonstrated.

Stimulus equivalence problems may also arise on a more subtle level when the researcher and target population speak the same language and national differences are less obvious (in the case, for example, of a U.S. researcher studying Australian managers). As with the emic-etic distinction, awareness of possible problems is a precondition for dealing with translation and stimulus equivalence problems.

SUMMARY

Despite the difficulties involved in international research, the need for research to assist managers and HRM practitioners remains. As Laurent[19] has pointed out:

> Many organizations are indeed confronted with the issues of managing human resources internationally. "Human Resource Managers" in such organizations are entitled to expect "Professors of HRM" to provide some useful insight on such processes. Yet these new international processes are so complex and so poorly defined and ill-understood at the moment that superficiality remains the mark of most treatments . . . . If the field of HRM is in a stage of adolescence, International HRM is still at the infancy stage.

These difficulties are not insurmountable, and as more managers and academics become aware of the many problems involved in international research, we should see progress in the field.

NOTES

1. H. Schollhammer, "Current Research in International and Comparative Management Issues," *Management International Review*, Vol. 15, No. 2–3 (1975) pp. 29–40.

2. See N. Adler, "Cross-Cultural Management Research: The Ostrich and the Trend," *Academy of Management Review*, Vol. 8 (1983) pp. 226–232.

3. Ibid.

4. C. Geertz, *The Interpretation of Cultures* (New York: Basic Books, 1973).

5. See R. S. Bhagat and S. J. McQuaid, "Role of Subjective Culture in Organizations: A Review and Directions for Future Research," *Journal of Applied Psychology*, Vol. 67 (1982) pp. 653–685; K. H. Roberts, "On Looking at an Elephant: An Evaluation of Cross-Cultural Research Related to Organizations," *Psychological Bulletin*, Vol. 74 (1970) pp. 327–350; and H. C. Triandis and R. W. Brislin, "Cross-Cultural Psychology," *American Psychologist*, Vol. 39 (1984) pp. 1006–1016.

6. Bhagat and McQuaid, "Role of Subjective Culture," p. 653.

7. J. W. Berry, "Introduction to Methodology," in *Handbook of Cross-Cultural Psychology, Vol. 2: Methodology*, ed. H. C. Triandis and J. W. Berry (Boston: Allyn & Bacon, 1980).

8. See Triandis and Brislin, "Cross-Cultural Psychology."

9. See G. Hofstede, "The Cultural Relativity of Organizational Practices and Theories," *Journal of International Business Studies*, Vol. 14, No. 2 (1983) pp. 75–89.

10. F. Harbison, "Management in Japan," in *Management in the Industrial World: An International Analysis*, ed. F. Harbison and C. A. Myers (New York: McGraw-Hill, 1959), p. 254.

11. T. S. Kuhn, *The Structure of Scientific Revolution*, 2nd ed. (Chicago, Ill.: University of Chicago Press, 1962).

12. J. D. Child, "Culture, Contingency and Capitalism in the Cross-National Study of Organizations," in *Research in Organizational Behavior*, Vol. 3, ed. L. L. Cummings and B. M. Staw (Greenwich, Conn.: JAI Publishers, 1981).

13. See Bhagat and McQuaid, "Role of Subjective Culture"; D. T. Campbell and J. Stanley, *Experimental and Quasi-Experimental Design for Research* (Chicago: Rand-McNally, 1966); and R. S. Malpass, "Theory and Method in Cross-Cultural Psychology," *American Psychologist*, Vol. 32 (1977) pp. 1069–1079.

14. Malpass, "Theory and Method," p. 1071.

15. See L. Kelley and R. Worthley, "The Role of Culture in Comparative Management: A Cross-Cultural Perspective," *Academy of Management Journal*, Vol. 24 (1981) pp. 164–173; and P. J. Dowling and T. W. Nagel, "Nationality and Work Attitudes: A Study of Australian and American Business Majors," *Journal of Management*, Vol. 12 (1986) pp. 121–128 for further discussion of this point.

16. Triandis and Brislin, "Cross-Cultural Psychology."

17. See R. Brislin, *Translation: Applications and Research* (New York: Gardner Press, 1976) for a review of this literature.

18. O. Werner and D. Campbell, "Translating, Working Through Interpreters, and the Problem of Decentering," in *A Handbook of Method in Cultural Anthropology*, ed. R. Naroll and R. Cohen (New York: Natural History Press, 1970).

19. A. Laurent, "The Cross-Cultural Puzzle of International Human Resource Management," *Human Resource Management*, Vol. 25 (1986) pp. 91–102.

Glossary*

As interest in international Human Resource Management (IHRM) has grown, there are concepts and ideas that are new and different from traditional domestic HRM. A *lingua franca* or common language is developing to facilitate communication about these new and different ideas and concepts.

Unfortunately, it becomes increasingly difficult for HR professionals and academics new to the IHRM field to understand and/or participate in the dialogue. Also, if there is not precision and consistency in the terms and terminology, even those in the IHRM field can become confused.

This list of IHRM terms is neither exhaustive nor rigorously scientific. If does have, however, many more terms and concepts than introduced in the chapters. As such it is a supplement as well as a glossary.

To avoid duplicative information, the definitions of the "terms" are grouped into major functional subjective areas as outlined in the list on the following page:

---

*This glossary was prepared by Patrick Morgan and is used here with his permission. According to the author:

"Three years ago I wrote down any **term** I heard or read that was unique to IHRM or relatively uncommon to traditional domestic HR operations. Approximately 250 terms were identified and a short **definition** and/or explanation for each term was developed.

Additionally, a search was made for a **print reference** for each term. Approximately twenty Personnel/HR/International management publications were reviewed to locate where more detail and perhaps additional reference material could be obtained on each term/subject. Print references for 75 percent of the terms have been located. References for most of the remaining terms exist, but frequently these are in publications or newsletters not widely available."

1. Planning
2. Recruitment and Selection
   a. Transfers/Repatriation
3. Training and Development
4. Labor Relations
5. Compensation and Benefits
   a. Administrative Issues
   b. Direct Compensation
   c. Indirect Compensation
   d. Benefit Plans
6. Travel
   a. Safety and Security
7. Operations
8. Government Relations
   a. Terms
   b. Visas
9. Dependent Relations

Planning

Assignment Status refers to whether an expatriate employee is accompanied by spouse and dependents on an international assignment. The types of assignment generally include:

Bachelor Status (see "Single Status")

Married Status the employee's spouse and dependent children are with the employee at the assignment location.

Family Status (as above)

Single Status the employee (married or not) does not have the spouse or dependents at the assignment location. Typically, only accommodation is provided.

Camp Status a special type of single status normally in remote locations, where employer provides messing, meals, laundry, etc., i.e., in a camp in addition to accommodation.

Critical Path a scheduling technique used to analyze a complex series of interconnected actions. The technique can be used to streamline lengthy recruiting and processing activity for international assignments. There are four broad employment approaches used internationally:

Ethnocentric approach reflects home-country bias in selecting candidates.

Geocentric approach selects best candidates on a worldwide global basis without any bias to any particular country.

Polycentric approach reflects a host-country bias in selecting employees.

Regiocentric approach selects best candidates on a regional basis without bias to any particular country in that region.

Recruitment and Selection

Employee Categories refers to the various types of employees. Some of the examples of employee categories include:

Expatriate (Expat) normally a professional/managerial employee moved from one country to, and for employment in, another country.

Female Expatriate Manager (as above)

Foreign Managers in the U.S. an "expatriate" in the U.S. where the U.S. is the host-country and the manager's home-country is outside of the U.S.

Foreign National frequently refers to the special case of a non-U.S. citizen assigned to the United States as an expatriate.

Indigenous Employee an alternate term for "local national/national" not often used because of prejudice concerns.

Inpatriate Foreign Manager in the U.S. Can also be used for U.S. expatriates returning to an assignment in the U.S.

International Staff expatriate employees from home-countries other than the U.S.

Local Hire an employee hired in-country for work in that country. Often has the special meaning that the employee is not a national of that country, i.e., an American hired in country X for employment in country X. However, the American's employment package is that of a local national, not a U.S. expatriate.

Local National/National an employee hired for employment in his or her own country.

PCN Parent-Country National.

HCN   Host-Country National.

TCNs   Third-Country Nationals; often refers to expatriate employees who are not U.S. citizens, but citizens of a "third" country.

Cadre   (France) a categorization approach (similar to U.S. exempt/non-exempt) that is a major determinant on compensation and benefit programs.

Employment Agreement   1) the written document defining the employer/employee relationship, 2) an arrangement for recruitment services with an external employment agency.

Employment Conditions   the compensation terms applicable to an assignment such as compensation uplifts, allowances, and paid absences.

Employment Contract   (see "Employment Agreement")

Host-Country   The country in which the assignment/employment is performed.

International Selection   the process by which candidates for overseas assignments are identified and reviewed.

Zaibatsu   (Japan) family tradition of becoming an apprentice at a young age and learning from a master for a long period.

Transfers/Repatriation

Assignment   refers to the period of time an employee is an expatriate. Special types include:

Business Trip   normally for a short period, generally less than one month in duration.

Extended Business Trip   normally longer than one month and maybe up to two to three months' duration.

Foreign Assignment   additional emphasis that the assignment is at an overseas location rather than domestic.

Permanent Assignment   in very few cases is an assignment truly "permanent." In most cases, an assignment of one or more years' duration is called "permanent."

Temporary Assignment   refers to a shorter assignment period of longer than 2 to 3 months, but normally shorter than one year in duration.

Assignment Completion   refers to the process of closing out an assignment and returning to the home-country and/or point-of-origin.

Culture Shock   the impact on employees and dependents when they arrive at a foreign location and begin to adjust and assimilate to the new location and its culture.

Expatriate Failure   occurs when, for whatever reason, an expatriate fails to complete the anticipated assignment period.

Failure Rates   turnover rate for employees.

Orientation   the system of preparing employees and dependents for their overseas assignment.

Pre-departure Briefing or Counseling   "Orientation" conducted prior to departure for an international assignment.

Processing   all the activities necessary to arrange for an employee and dependents to depart and arrive at their assignment location. Included are such activities as passports, visas, household effects moving and storage, airline ticketing, vaccinations, etc.

Re-entry Shock   the cultural readjustments necessary when a person returns to his or her home country.

Retrenchment   a lay-off situation also referred to sometimes as redundancy.

Repatriation   the process of return to the home country at completion of assignment.

Reverse Culture Shock   (see "Re-entry Shock")

Safe Arrival Notification   when employees/dependents have travelled to a remote assignment location, it is a common practice to advise family and friends in the home country of their safe arrival at the assignment location.

Training and Development

Cross-cultural Training   process of sensitizing employees and dependents to the cultural differences between host- and home-country cultures.

Cultural Empathy   an awareness of differences in culture and how those differences impact society and business.

Culturally-Based Discrimination   normally the result of a lack of cultural awareness and cultural empathy.

Cultural Assimilation training program to assist employees and dependents to live in a foreign culture.

Cultural Orientation training program to familiarize employee and dependents on cultural issues.

Environmental Briefing training program on physical aspects of the location/country of assignment; climate, language, politics, etc.

Field Experience training program on living/working in a foreign environment.

Language Training preparation of expatriate employees and dependents for the host-country language.

Localization the process of replacing expatriates (normally higher cost) with local national employees.

Sensitivity Training training program to increase awareness of cultural issues.

Labor Relations

ACAS Advisory, Conciliation and Arbitration Service within U.K.

Arbitration a process whereby a neutral third party reviews employer and labor representative input on an item under dispute and renders a binding decision.

Conciliation a process whereby a neutral third party reviews employer and labor representative input on an item under dispute and attempts to have both parties agree to a compromise arrangement.

Labor Agreements terms and conditions agreed upon between an employer and unions that cover the company's operations.

Shunto spring wage offensive in Japan.

Taiso daily physical exercise routine practiced by many Japanese employers.

Pendulum Arbitration a process where an arbitrator has to choose between the last offer and the last claim by the parties. A compromise position is not permitted.

Tea Money (Australia) an allowance under a union agreement to provide money to allow the worker to buy refreshments (tea, etc.) for an approved rest break.

Compensation and Benefits

Administrative Issues

Balance Sheet Approach is a compensation approach that identifies the gains and losses of a particular assignment due to taxes, cost-of-living, etc. and attempts to even out windfalls and shortfalls to achieve the desired incentive level.

Base Salary the salary the employee would receive for the same job in his or her own home country for a normal workweek/month.

Base Workweek the length of a normal workweek in the employee's home country, i.e., 5 days/40 hours, 6 days/48 hours, $4\frac{1}{2}$ days/$37\frac{1}{2}$ hours.

Bi-lateral Tax Agreement between the U.S. and a foreign government which defines the personal income tax arrangements for U.S. expatriates assigned to that foreign country.

Bona-Fide Foreign Resident a term in the IRS tax code that relates to Section 911 and qualification for the Foreign Earned Income exclusion.

CPI Consumer Price Index.

Deferred Compensation is earned but paid at a later date, through a variety of different arrangements, to reduce the income tax impact.

Devaluation occurs when the value of a particular currency erodes against another currency.

Dual Employment Contracts an employee resides and works in one country but travels to and works in another country. Two employment contracts cover this arrangement.

Exchange Rates the value of a particular currency against another currency.

FIRP the Foreign Income Information Returns Program is a system where the tax authorities of certain foreign nations agree to send IRS available information on the income earned in those nations by U.S. expatriates.

Foreign Earned Income Exclusion provision of Section 911 of the IRS code allowing the deduction of certain income earned through employment overseas.

Foreign Housing Cost when the employer pays or reimburses the housing costs for a U.S. expatriate, there is a tax implication.

Foreign Source Income   refers to income/compensation paid to an employee outside of the U.S.

Foreign Tax Credit   because U.S. citizens/residents are taxed on their worldwide income, expatriates often pay foreign tax and the U.S. government allows a credit against a U.S. tax liability.

Goods and Services   that portion of income that an employee spends on items such as food, medical, recreation, transportation.

Housing Exclusion   provisions of the IRS code relating to the manner in which housing costs are reported for tax purposes.

Hypothetical Tax   a theoretical income tax liability calculation based on assumptions on income, dependents, and deductions.

Incentives   the intended levels of additional compensation for undertaking an international assignment.

Market Basket   a selection of typical shopping items used to compare cost-of-living differences between host and home countries.

National Salary   for expatriates compensated in a host-country approach, often there is a need to develop a hypothetical home-country base salary for benefit plan purposes.

Overbase Compensation   additional payments over and above base salary to compensate for hardship, danger, extended workweek, etc.

Physical Presence   relates to Section 911 of the IRS code and qualification for the foreign earned income exclusion.

Rest Day   in some countries, the compensation paid is for a 7-day period of which one or two days are paid rest days. In other countries, compensation is based on an "hours-worked" approach.

Section 401(K)   section of the IRS code that allows a salary reduction/deferred taxation arrangement.

Section 911   section of the IRS code that contains the foreign earned income provisions.

Spendable Income   that amount of net pay left after deductions for taxes and benefits.

Split Payments   where compensation is delivered through a combination of delivery methods and/or currencies.

Split Pay   where pay is delivered in a combination of host and home-country currencies.

Split Payroll   where an employee is on two payrolls, with each paying only a portion of the salary, to reduce income taxes in the host country.

Tax Equalization   an expatriate is charged a hypothetical tax, and the employer then pays all other host- and home-country income taxes.

Tax Protection   employee pays host- and home-country taxes, and the employer reimburses excess taxes over agreed figure.

Thirteenth Month   compensation bonus-type arrangement where one month's extra salary is paid once a year.

U.S. Source Income   refers to income/compensation paid within the U.S.

VAT   (U.K., Europe) Value Added Tax, very similar to a sales tax.

Direct Compensation

Aguinaldo   (Mexico) a mandatory annual bonus of 15 to 30 days' pay, normally paid at Christmas time.

Antiquidates   (Venezuela) a half a month bonus for service indemnity.

Cesantia   (Venezuela) a half a month bonus for termination indemnity.

Completion Allowance   additional compensation paid annually or at completion of assignment. Often used at remote hardship locations to encourage employees to remain for the full assignment period.

Convenios   (Spain) annual salary increases.

Danger Pay   at assignment locations where there is physical danger (war, etc.), often a special additional salary payment is made.

Expatriate Allowance   payment to employee for undertaking an international assignment.

Expatriation Premium   (as above)

Extended Workweek Premium   to minimize the number of expatriate employees and their associated costs (i.e., instead of 3 expats working 40 hours a week, using 2 expats working 60 hours), often the normal scheduled workweek is increased and additional payment made.

Foreign Service Premium   (see "Expatriate Allowance")

Hardship Allowance   at locations that are less desirable and have more hardship, normally additional payment is made over and above the expatriation premium.

Salvencia   (Venezuela) a 20% tax on temporary assignments.

177

Syndicato   (Brazil) salary indexation tied to inflation rate.

Trienios   (Spain) salary increases mandated by Spanish law at three-year intervals.

Uplifts   payments often expressed as percents of base salary, to compensate employee for expatriation, hardship, danger, extended work-week and assignment completion.

Utilidates   (Venezuela) two months' bonus.

Indirect Compensation

Assumed Shelter Cost   in calculating a cost differential allowance often a hypothetical or assumed cost of housing in either or both the host and home country is used.

At-Post Education   where dependent children can attend educational facilities at the assignment location.

Away-From-Post Education   when adequate schooling facilities are not available for dependent children at the assignment location, they frequently attend boarding schools in another country.

Cacabatro   (Algeria) vacation accrual plan.

Correspondence Allowance   where adequate schooling is not available at an assignment location, or a dependent child has special educational needs, correspondence courses are often used and reimbursed.

Cost Differential   a payment to compensate employee for differences in living costs (housing, goods, and services) between host and home countries.

Cost-of-Living Allowance   (see "Cost Differential")

Country-of-Origin   country from which employee originally departed and to which employee is returned at the end of assignment.

Education Allowance   payment to employee for increased education costs for dependent children.

Enroute Expenses   reimbursement for hotel, taxi, meals, porters and other incident costs associated with traveling between the home country and the assignment location.

Fringe Benefits   various forms of indirect compensation (also see "Perquisite").

Furnishing Allowance   reimbursement for cost of furnishing accommodations at the assignment location.

Home Leave   paid round-trip from assignment location to point and/or country of origin. Frequency often tied to degree of hardship at assignment location.

Household Effects   usually refers to home-country furniture which is usually stored in country of origin and a portion shipped to assignment location.

Housing Allowance   payment for accommodation costs at assignment location.

Living Allowance   (see "Cost Differential")

LVs   (U.K.) Luncheon Vouchers — has similarity to "food stamps" redeemable at restaurants.

Negative Differentials   situation where a calculation for an allowance such as a cost differential shows negative, i.e., costs of assignment location are less than home-country costs.

Per Diem Allowance   a flat daily allowance for travel expenses (see "Enroute Expenses").

Perqs   (see "Perquisite")

Perquisite   indirect compensation delivered in a form that has less income tax impact on employee and employer, i.e., company car.

Personal Effects   clothing and other personal items that are shipped, under a personal effects allowance, to the assignment location.

Point-of-Hire   location/city where the employee was hired.

Point-of-Origin   location to which employee is returned at end of assignment (see "Country-of-Origin").

R&R   at remote and hardship locations and/or where an employee is on an unaccompanied basis, provision is made to leave the assignment location for a short break.

Rest & Recreation Leave   (see "R&R")

Ramadan   one of the Hijrah calendar months in which Moslems fast from sunrise to sunset.

Relocation Allowance   paid to assist an employee relocate from home country to host country and also upon return.

Settling-In Allowance   reimbursement for living costs at the assignment location until the arrival of personal and household effects shipment and movement into permanent accommodation.

Severance Pay in many countries at termination, a redundancy or final separation payment is required by law.

Travel Time often a number of days pay is allowed for travel to and from the assignment location from the home country.

Utilities Allowance sometimes a payment, separate from the housing allowance, is made for local utility costs; water, power, sewage, telephone, gas.

Benefit Plans

Annuity Plan a retirement plan that provides payment of normally a fixed amount on a monthly, quarterly, or annual basis.

Casoran (Algeria) social insurance program.

Dirigenti (Italy) a social insurance contribution for managers.

GOSI (Saudi Arabia) a social insurance program.

Long Service Leave (Australia) after a period of service with an employer (approximately 10 to 15 years), the employee is entitled to a paid leave of absence of approximately 3 to 6 months.

Provident Fund a retirement savings type plan common to many countries.

Savings Plans a retirement type plan where the employer withholds and "saves" a portion of the employee's pay.

Superannuation a retirement type plan common to many countries.

Totalization Agreement between the U.S. government and another foreign government covers arrangements on social security contributions and payments for their respective nationals in the other country.

War Risk Insurance a special type of corporate insurance used when other insurance coverage lapses because of declared or undeclared war.

Travel

Airport Tax some international airports impose an airport or departure tax for people departing the country.

ETA/ETD estimated time of arrival; estimated time of departure.

Excess Baggage that amount over and above the airline's "free" accompanied baggage allowance—often on weight basis.

FCU   Foreign Currency Unit system used by airlines to price tickets in different international currencies.

Health Certificate   used to record vaccinations against certain infectious diseases such as cholera, typhoid, smallpox.

Jet Lag   body clock disorientation caused by crossing time zones.

MCO   Miscellaneous Charges Order. These are credit notes issued by airlines.

Meet and Greet   for the first-time arrivals at foreign airports, often a company representative is available at the airport to assist in customs and immigration formalities.

NTSC   television transmission and reception format used in the U.S.

PAL   television transmission and reception format used in many European countries.

SECAM   television transmission and reception format used in some European countries.

Shot Book   (see "Health Certificate")

Transit Accommodations   where the assignment location is remote from a large urban area/international airport, it may be necessary to stay overnight, continuing travel the next day.

Vaccination Book   (see "Health Certificate")

Safety and Security

Contingency Plans   back-up plan of action in case of emergency.

Emergency Plans   usually cover protection of expatriate employees, dependents, and company property/records in case of civil disorder or national disaster.

Medivac   the evacuation of a sick employee and/or dependent from the assignment location to another location/country for emergency medical treatment.

Milton's   disinfectant solution used to treat fruit and vegetables of questionable origin and/or cleanliness.

Survival Kit   at the assignment location, pending the arrival of household and personal effects shipments, interim equipment is supplied.

Terrorism   includes concerns on travel and security at the assignment location.

Operations

Dating Systems   around the world, there are a variety of systems in use. Some countries use month/day/year, others use day/month/year. To avoid confusion as to whether 2/3/89 is February or March, many internationalists always use at least three alpha characters to eliminate confusion about the month, i.e., "3 FEB '89."

Global   a corporation offering uniform products worldwide because it's in a truly global industry. Also called a *transnational corporation.*

Gregorian Calendar   is the traditional 12-month, January through December, solar calendar.

Hijrah Calendar   an 11-month calendar used in the Middle East Islamic countries which is based on a lunar, rather than solar calendar; 1987 in the Gregorian calendar is approximately the year 1407 in the Hijrah calendar.

Joint Venture   an arrangement where a number of different companies associate to form a new legal entity to pursue or perform a specific objective. In addition to pooling resources, it allows the participating companies to spread the risk.

MNC   multinational corporation. A corporation operating facilities in several different countries of the world. Also called an *international firm.*

Government Relations

Terms

Consularization   process whereby a consular office endorses a document with a stamp attesting to the translation and/or validity of a document, i.e., college degree.

CONUS   the continental United States, i.e., the 48 contiguous states excluding Hawaii and Alaska.

Fiscal Clearance   prior to a foreign resident departing a host country, many countries require a document issued by the local Tax and/or Treasury department verifying that host-country income taxes have been paid.

Foreign Corrupt Practices Act   the U.S. Foreign Corrupt Practices Act of 1977 prohibits payments to foreign government officials.

International Driving Permit   Approximately 160 countries honor the 1949 United Nations' Convention on Road Traffic and agree that a permit issued in the home country is valid to drive in the host country.

Labor Court   in some countries, there are special courts established to handle employee complaints on local labor law violations.

Labor Law   in some countries, the law applicable to employees has been codified into a consolidated labor law.

MOL   In many countries this is the Ministry of Labor (Labour).

Notarization   process whereby an authorized person attests to and confirms the validity of a document or signature.

Police Clearance   document required by many countries, prior to issuing the visa, that confirms employee does not have criminal record in the place of previous residence.

Quitas Fiscal   (Algeria) a clearance required to leave the country (see "Fiscal Clearance").

Visas

In *overseas* countries, there are a variety of *visa* types and formalities as follows:

> *Dependent Visa*   permits a family to accompany or join employee in country of assignment.
>
> *Exit Visa*   permits a foreign resident to leave the host country.
>
> *Exit/Re-entry Visa*   permits a foreign resident to leave and then re-enter the host country.
>
> *Landed Immigrant*   a permanent residence visa for Canada.
>
> *Multiple Entry Visa*   permits multiple entries to a country without the need to obtain a new visa each visit.
>
> *Residency Visa*   permits entry and allows person to take up permanent residency in the country.
>
> *Single Entry Visa*   permits a one-time entry into a country. Another visa is required for any further visits.
>
> *Work Permit*   authorizes paid employment in a country.
>
> *Work Visa*   authorizes entry into a country to take up paid employment.

U.S. Visa and immigration formalities involve a number of specialized terms as follows:

B-1 Visa   visitor on business visa.

F-1 Visa   student visa.

Green Card/Green Card Holder   U.S. resident alien.

H-1 Visa   temporary worker of distinguished merit and ability.

I-94 Form   record of entry into the U.S. issued at port of arrival and attached to the passport.

Immigrant Visa   a visa issued for entrance for permanent residence in the U.S.A.

INS   Immigration and Naturalization Service.

IRCA   Immigration Reform and Control Act of 1986.

J-1 Visa   exchange visitor.

L-1 Visa   intra-company transfer.

Non-Immigrant Visa   a visa issued for entrance and temporary residence in the U.S.

Resident Alien   an individual previously admitted on an immigrant visa and who is now a permanent resident of the U.S.

Visa Reference   six categories of priority for issuance of a U.S. immigrant visa.

White Book   issued to green card holders going outside the U.S. on an international assignment to document intent to return and remain as U.S. resident aliens.

Dependent Relations

Dependents   the spouse and children of the expatriate employee.

Pets   there are various regulations on the transportation and entry of pets into foreign countries.

Servants   household help at the assignment location.

Index